No Place For a Boy

A Life at Harland & Wolff

No Place For a Boy

A Life at Harland & Wolff

Tom McCluskie MBE

TEMPUS

To the Oul Hands

First published 2007

Tempus Publishing Limited
The Mill, Brimscombe Port,
Stroud, Gloucestershire, GL5 2QG
www.tempus-publishing.com

British Library Cataloguing in Publication Data.
A catalogue record for this book is available from the British Library.

ISBN 978 0752 4216 3

Typesetting and origination by Tempus Publishing Limited
Printed in Great Britain

Contents

Introduction

The city and port of Belfast, Northern Ireland, has been associated with the building of ships for well over 300 years, with the first vessels recorded as having been completed in 1663. Sadly, this fine tradition of craftsmanship and excellence in the field of marine engineering has now come to an end and vessels are no longer being built by Harland & Wolff Ltd, at one time arguably the finest and most famous shipbuilder in the world. The slipways and building berths that saw the construction of such magnificent vessels as the RMS *Titanic*, *Canberra* and *Southern Cross* now lie derelict and forlorn, nothing more than silent witnesses to the demise of a once mighty industrial complex and a golden age of shipbuilding.

There are many reasons for the decline and fall of this historic company and not all of them are as straightforward as they would first appear. In the course of this book I will touch upon some of the more shadowy aspects behind the slow but nonetheless deliberate destruction of this great company. To understand and appreciate the magnitude of what may best be described as a wanton act of industrial vandalism, it would perhaps be useful at this stage to provide some words of clarification on the history of a company once described as the 'Shipbuilder to the World'. In chronicling these events it has been necessary to protect the identity of certain individuals to avoid any potential embarrassment to, or degradation of, their reputations. Furthermore, the timing and chronological order surrounding certain events has been abridged for the sake of clarity, however the veracity of these events remains intact.

The river Lagan flows through the heart of the City of Belfast and provided the foundation and lifeblood for the steady rise in the city's prosperity by allowing merchants and traders ready access to ocean-going vessels. The establishment of this burgeoning commercial trade led to a need for some sort of repair facility to service and maintain these vessels which, over time, would evolve into actual shipbuilding operations and eventually into the formation of the massive Harland & Wolff shipbuilding complex of shipyards and engineering works. However, before this leviathan would emerge there would be several false starts and many trials and tribulations along the way.

Thanks to much environmental effort by various bodies, the river Lagan today is a clean and relatively straight waterway far removed from its original course which meandered in a narrow and twisting manner through the city in the eighteenth century. At that time the ever-increasing use of the river for commerce and trade prompted the establishment of the Belfast Harbour Commissioners in 1785; this body took the grandiose title 'The Corporation for Preserving and Improving the Port and Harbour of the City of Belfast'.

This august body of gentlemen, comprised in the main of merchants and traders, immediately instituted an ambitious programme of improvements to the quays and wharves along the banks of the river as well as straightening and widening the waterway itself in several locations by means of two massive straight cuts directly towards the mouth of Belfast Lough and the sea beyond. The construction work involved the excavation and dumping of several million tons of spoil and debris at the mouth of the river along the eastern shoreline.

The massive amount of material deposited eventually formed a huge island which, in time, would become known as Queen's Island in honour of Queen Victoria who would officially open the newly reconstructed port facilities in August 1849. This feverish activity had not gone unnoticed by industrialists on the mainland of Great Britain and the magnificent improvements to the port facilities soon attracted the attention of William Ritchie, an established shipbuilder from the fishing port of Saltcoats on the Ayrshire coast of Scotland. Ritchie had taken the opportunity to visit Belfast in 1791 and had been tremendously impressed by the new port facilities, offering as they did the potential for the expansion of his long-established shipbuilding business. He quickly drew up plans for the establishment of a new shipbuilding yard to be located on the west bank of the river Lagan and was jubilant to receive a warm and enthusiastic welcome for his proposal from the Harbour Commissioners. He was even more delighted to be offered, in return for his investment, the provision and exclusive use of a docking platform on which vessels could be raised out of the water for hull cleaning and repair. The arrival of William Ritchie and his shipbuilding operations in Belfast laid the foundation stones of a tradition of shipbuilding and marine engineering which would lead, some sixty years later, to the ambition of Edward Harland to develop his own fledgling venture, Harland & Wolff, into the greatest and most famous shipbuilding company in the world.

Edward Harland was born in May 1831 in Scarborough, Yorkshire, the sixth child of Dr William Harland, a successful and well-respected medical practitioner. Dr Harland had also established something of a reputation as a talented inventor, having designed, built and patented his own version of a steam carriage in 1827. From his earliest years young Edward had also displayed a talent for engineering and, by his own admission, frequently neglected his academic studies, preferring to watch engineers at work and often joining in their activities. This is perhaps not quite so surprising when one considers that his father was a close personal friend and confidant of the famous scientist and engineer George Stephenson, probably better known as the father of the steam engine. It is little wonder then, given such illustrious mentors, that Edward Harland should see himself in the mould of Stephenson and that he would also establish a formidable reputation of his own as a renowned engineer and inventor.

While his father harboured hopes that Edward would soon tire of his obsession and return to his studies as a barrister, likewise Edward remained just as determined to become a professional engineer and in 1846, having completed his grammar school education, he promptly accepted an apprenticeship with Robert Stephenson & Co. of Newcastle.

During this apprenticeship Edward became deeply interested in the design of ships and the practicalities of shipbuilding. A particular preoccupation he developed at this time was with the enormous loss of life among seafarers; in the summer of 1850 he produced a revolutionary design for a new type of lifeboat which would have a propeller at each end. However, much to his disappointment his idea was rejected as impractical and too costly to provide.

Undeterred however, he continued to develop his ideas and designs for sea-going vessels and returned to his studies with renewed vigour and optimism. As his apprenticeship progressed Edward had become friendly with Gustav Christian Schwabe, a wealthy merchant born in Hamburg in 1815. Gustav's eldest sister, Fanny, was married to her brother's closest friend Moritz Wolff, with whom she had two sons, Gustav Wilhelm, born in 1834 and George Moritz Otto, born in 1840.

Gustav Wolff had arranged to leave the family home at the tender age of fourteen to live with his uncle Gustav Schwabe in Liverpool, where he was to attend Liverpool college to study engineering and take up an apprenticeship with Joseph Whitworth & Co. of Manchester. The young Gustav rapidly established a reputation as an excellent engineer and was honoured to be selected to represent Whitworth & Co. at the Paris engineering exhibition in 1855. In 1856, ever keen to improve his engineering skills, Gustav joined B. Goodfellows Ltd of Hyde as a draughtsman. However, the post would prove to be short-lived, as later in the same year he accepted a position with the Belfast shipbuilder Robert Hickson & Co. as a junior manager. The appointments to such positions had little to do with academic ability, rather they were only provided to the sons of wealthy parents who wished to learn a business in which they hoped to eventually become directors. Gustav's move to Belfast also resulted in the happy coincidence of meeting and working with Edward Harland, whom he had known for some time as a friend of his father.

Edward Harland had himself arrived in Belfast during the summer of 1854 to take up an appointment as shipyard manager to Robert Hickson & Co. Upon his arrival Edward had immediately taken charge of the only vessel then undergoing construction, a sailing clipper named *Khersonese* which was already considerably behind schedule and long overdue for completion. Edward recognised several areas where progress could be made and introduced new working methods to recover as much of the lost time as possible, although these new working arrangements were not universally welcomed by the workforce. Much to his chagrin he discovered that Hickson had been paying wages far above the usual rate and had accepted shoddy and inferior craftsmanship from his employees. Edward immediately slashed the wages and introduced a system of work inspection, a forerunner of today's modern quality control procedures, whereby inferior or unsatisfactory work was rejected and was to be repaired at the craftsman's own expense. To further improve discipline and safety he immediately prohibited all smoking in the workplace or on board the vessel and demanded that no employee was to stand with his hands in his pockets for any reason whatsoever.

Not surprisingly, these draconian but nevertheless necessary measures resulted in the workers immediately going on strike. Edward responded to this provocation by immediately sacking the entire workforce and replacing them with labour recruited from Scotland. These shock tactics rapidly had the desired effect and, after a suitable face-saving period, the striking workers returned and grudgingly accepted their new terms and conditions.

Unbeknown to the workforce, however, was the fact that Edward Harland was facing much more serious difficulties of his own. In the spring of 1855 the Ulster Banking Co., long concerned at the fiscal performance of Hickson's operations, finally lost all patience with him and proceeded to foreclose on all their outstanding business and personal loans. This disastrous state of affairs resulted in Edward having to fund the daily operating costs of the yard out of his own pocket, while at the same time frantically trying to reach some sort of accommodation with the yard's creditors. Desperately struggling to keep the yard in operation, he unexpectedly found himself being offered some much-needed help.

Thomas Toward & Co. was a long-established shipbuilding company on the river Tyne in Newcastle, where Edward had been employed for a year in 1853. Following the death of the founder Thomas Toward in 1855, the senior foreman, William Houston, and a large number of skilled craftsmen had moved to Belfast to help complete the now massively delayed *Khersonese*. This influx of expert labour made the production vastly more efficient while the quality of work improved beyond all recognition, with the consequence that Edward gained sufficient breathing space to sort out the financial mess he had inherited from Hickson. To assist in the reconstruction of the company Edward appointed Gustav Wolff as his personal assistant in 1857, and together the two friends proceeded to assemble a rescue package for the company. Despite the numerous difficulties and tremendous pressure applied by the creditors, on 21 September 1858 Hickson formally offered Edward Harland the opportunity to purchase his entire interest in the shipyard for the princely sum of £5,000. Eager to avail himself of what he considered a golden opportunity, Edward turned for to his old friend (and Wolff's uncle) Gustav Schwabe for advice and support. With Schwabe's financial backing and encouragement, Edward Harland duly purchased the entire shipbuilding enterprise of Robert Hickson on 1 November 1858. His first action on assuming control was to change the name of the company to Edward James Harland & Co.

Edward began his shipbuilding operations by quickly disposing of the original site of the Hickson yard and taking out a lease on an area of land on the new Queen's Island.

This allowed him to design and lay out a yard to his own exact requirements while the additional land area also gave him the freedom to expand further if necessary. Edward Harland, now in complete control of his own destiny, rapidly expanded his shipbuilding operations while simultaneously enhancing his reputation for quality and reliability. One of his key actions at this time was to appoint Gustav Wolff as Chief Draughtsman in the new company and charge him with reorganising the drawing offices into a more cohesive and efficient operation.

Wolff succeeded in this task to such an extent that within a few months he had, in collaboration with Edward, produced a portfolio of new and innovative vessel designs. Edward soon realised that in Wolff he had discovered a kindred spirit who shared his dreams and ideals, especially those concerning the development of modern iron steam ships. It was no surprise therefore when, on 11 April 1861, the two friends formally entered into an official partnership by establishing the renowned shipbuilding and engineering company of Harland & Wolff Ltd, which officially commenced operations on 1 January 1862. The company would soon become recognised as a world leader in vessel construction with its introduction of innovative and technologically advanced designs for vessels of all types. The reputation gained by the company for this excellence in design and construction was maintained right up to the day when shipbuilding operations finally ceased after some 137 years of operation. An illustration of the quality and strength of the vessels produced by a company may be found in the price paid for second-hand vessels built by it, or in the residual value of the vessel when it is eventually disposed of for scrap. Vessels built by Harland & Wolff routinely attract the highest resale or scrap value of comparable vessels, chiefly because their inherent strength and durability make them exceedingly difficult to break-up or destroy.

After Hickson had sold his interest in the shipyard to Harland, Edward swiftly set about the onerous task of convincing the major ship owners of the period that his designs were worth considering. However, Harland realised that his first task would be to establish his credentials as a shipbuilder of quality and reliability in his own right by producing sturdy vessels based on tried and trusted traditional designs. Over several years during his time under Hickson, Edward had managed to establish a reputation with John Bibby, the Liverpool ship owner, and so it was from Bibby that Edward Harland received his first shipbuilding order.

In April 1858 John Bibby signed a contract with Edward Harland for the construction of three iron vessels of approximately 1,500 tons each. They were to be named the *Venetian, Sicilian* and *Syrian* respectively. Each vessel was to be fitted with an auxiliary steam engine although, as the actual horsepower was less than the sail area, they would be classified as sailing ships. Such was Bibby's personal faith in Harland's abilities that he allowed Edward to construct these new vessels to his new hull design; a radical departure from the accepted standard of short-length and wide-beam. Harland's unique design adopted a much more radical concept for the hull; a long, slender hull on a narrow beam which permitted a greater tonnage capacity without the corresponding increase in vessel weight or the need for the greater power of an increased sail area. This revolutionary design proved to be astoundingly successful in service, producing greater voyage speeds than ever before as well as improved stability in heavy seas.

So, delighted at the commercial success of his new vessels, John Bibby consequently returned to Harland for a further series of sixteen vessels. Innovative as Edward's designs were they were still regarded with some caution, if not suspicion, by other ship owners less progressive than Bibby, with the result that Edward was forced to continue to refine and develop his ideas while undertaking contracts to build ships to the more traditional specifications, such as his fifth vessel, the classic barque *Jane Porter*. While sailing vessels were the accepted mode of vessel propulsion in the 1860s, the development of the steam engine as a method for powering a vessel was becoming ever more a consideration. Edward Harland, himself a fervent supporter of this new technology, found it increasingly difficult to combine the pressures of running what was quickly becoming a very successful shipbuilding company with the development of marine steam engines. However, thanks to his new partner and his pioneering skills in the adaptation of steam power for a marine environment, they would subsequently offer a significant contribution to the development of steam propulsion.

The adoption of steam as a method of powering a vessel was not quite as enthusiastically welcomed by the majority of ship owners as the partners would have hoped. Their ideas, while being generally accepted as feasible, were for the most part untried and, being naturally cautious and conservative in their approach to all things new, ship owners much preferred the 'wait and see' attitude to such new technology. Once again it fell to Bibby to come to the rescue of the partners by agreeing to try a steam engine as the primary method of propulsion in the two new vessels he intended to order from Harland & Wolff. Not entirely convinced by the partners' presentation and assurances, he also insisted that the conventional arrangement of sails be provided, just in case. The result of this hybrid arrangement was the appearance in 1861 of the striking *Grecian* and *Italian*, each embodying all that was new and innovative in vessel design and construction while still retaining a traditional profile and appearance. The revolutionary long and slim hull form, which became known throughout ship-owning circles as the 'Bibby coffin', or more correctly, and as preferred by Edward Harland, the 'Belfast bottom', was very much in evidence. The grace and power of these vessels enhanced the reputation of Harland & Wolff throughout the world as innovative and progressive shipbuilders. Ship owners soon began to follow the example set by John Bibby and approached Harland & Wolff for innovative designs for their new vessels.

This marked the beginning of the company's inexorable rise until it reached its peak in the 1920s and '30s, a truly 'golden age' for shipping. Now led by a dynamic Chairman in Lord Pirrie, Harland & Wolff had weathered the storm surrounding the loss of the RMS *Titanic* and had grown into the largest shipyard in the world, both in terms of production and physical size. Almost 65,000 people were employed directly by the company at its various locations across the United Kingdom, with satellite yards in Glasgow, Liverpool, London and Southampton. It also operated two massive engine-building works, the largest being in Belfast and the other located at Finneston in Glasgow. To complete the picture, an immense iron foundry situated beside the Belfast engine works produced the huge castings necessary for the ships under construction.

The partnership of Edward James Harland and Gustav Wolff changed the face of shipbuilding on a global scale; as the history of the company reflects, they were indeed 'Shipbuilders to the World'. Recognised throughout ship-owning circles as pioneering the march of technological progress, they produced such instantly recognisable and beautiful vessels as *Titanic*, *Southern Cross*, *Canberra* and HMS *Belfast*, which fired the opening salvoes on D-Day, 6 June 1944.

For the men who worked there, often in harsh and dangerous conditions, the pride they felt in the construction and completion of a 'Belfast boat' cannot easily be put into words. One simply had to be there, to be a part of it to truly understand the emotions and the camaraderie working in Harland & Wolff engendered among its employees. These were hard men working in a hard industry, yet nevertheless these employees experienced a tremendous sense of pride and achievement when a completed vessel departed her place of birth for the oceans of the world.

Similarly, the sudden loss of a vessel such as that of the RMS *Titanic* was felt as deeply as a personal tragedy. Such is the depth of emotion and pride felt in the completion of every vessel built by Harland & Wolff that it can only truly be appreciated or understood by those who have dedicated their lives to the company. It was into this world that I arrived as a fresh-faced youth eager to make my way in the world. Little could I have realised that, over the course of the next thirty-five years, I would succeed in becoming one of the youngest managers in the history of Harland & Wolff and play a major part in the production of the most expensive movie ever made by helping to reconstruct an almost full-scale replica of the RMS *Titanic* in a car park in an industrial estate in Mexico.

I later retired from Harland & Wolff after suffering a major stroke, but struggled to recover from its devastating effects and would go on to become the author of four books on the history of Harland & Wolff and many of the vessels they built, in particular a definitive study of the RMS *Titanic* and her sister ships. These books have gone on to become the accepted standard reference works on the subject matter and have enjoyed worldwide sales that have led to my being acknowledged as one of the world's leading experts on maritime history and the RMS *Titanic*. However, perhaps my most significant achievement was my struggle against tremendous opposition to preserve the historic archive of Harland & Wolff for future generations to study. Battling against inconceivable difficulties, which ranged from boardroom indifference to downright opposition from almost every quarter imaginable, the fight to preserve this unique and irreplaceable archive eventually took a terrible toll on my personal health and well-being.

Time and again the frustration and exasperation of being forced to act without any dependable measure of support or encouragement almost became too much to bear, and on several occasions I came close to giving up the unequal struggle in order to safeguard my own sanity.

Today this unique archive survives almost completely intact, distributed between various museums and agencies to ensure its continued preservation. In June 2004 I was surprised and delighted to be honoured by Her Majesty Queen Elizabeth II with the award of the MBE (Member of the Most Excellent Order of the British Empire), the citation reading: 'For services to maritime history and the RMS *Titanic*'. To be the recipient of this special honour, received in recognition of my efforts in preserving the maritime heritage of what was once one of the world's most important shipbuilding companies, was an acknowledgement that the country as a whole recognised what I had accomplished. On reflection I had come a long way from the back streets of Belfast and the fresh-faced but frightened youth bravely facing his first day in the mighty shipyard that was Harland & Wolff. Unbeknown to me at that precise moment, I was about to embark on a remarkable journey through life that would lead me into the depths of despair and heartbreak, and yet still provide me with moments of inspiration and joy unconfined.

In the course of my journey I would meet many wonderful people, larger than life characters unique to this special place, many of whom I would come to regard as personal friends and who would stand shoulder to shoulder with me in some of my darkest moments. Bonds of friendship forged so strong and deep as to be unbreakable, a bond so intense it is only truly understandable to those who have dedicated their lives to building the great ships that ply the oceans of the world.

Shipbuilding may have ceased forever on Queen's Island, bringing to a close a significant chapter in the history of world shipbuilding, but to have been a small part of that history is a singular honour and I consider myself privileged indeed to have been associated with some of the finest men I ever knew.

Chapter One

Unusually for early July, an icy wind was blowing along the little back street, whipping the chilly rain into a fury, each drop stinging like a razor-sharp needle upon the skin of anyone unfortunate enough to be outside facing the elements that morning. As I attempted to snuggle even deeper under the warm blankets and ignore the howling gale outside, I realised I was only kidding myself and very soon I would be forced to leave my snug cocoon and face whatever the day had to bring. To the world in general it was just another Monday, but for me this particular day was destined to be unlike any other Monday in my life thus far. This was indeed a very special Monday; this was the day that would become the first day of my career in Harland & Wolff and, although I couldn't have known it at the time, it would mark the start of a wonderful adventure. In the years to come I would run the gamut of every human emotion, from moments of joy and laughter to periods of great sadness and black despair. However, at that particular moment such thoughts were far from my youthful mind as I allowed myself to drift back into a blissful slumber, content in the knowledge that I had left my school days behind forever.

The previous Friday I had left the Boys Model Secondary School, a modern but nonetheless austere building perched high up on the slopes of Cave Hill, which overlooked the City of Belfast and river Lagan down to the beautiful dark, rolling hills of County Down beyond. More importantly, from my perspective, the classroom windows presented an excellent panorama of the Harland & Wolff shipyards far below, and I must admit to spending many hours gazing out of the window at the complex rather than paying full attention to my academic studies. My final day at school could not come quickly enough and I was delighted to at last be free of the drudgery of school life and anxious to make my own way in the world. Never a great scholar, I saw school as a necessary interference in life and one to be endured rather than enjoyed. From my earliest years I had always known I would follow my father into the shipyard, and consequently the efforts of the several careers masters to guide my youthful ideas onto other avenues were simply wasted on me, the strength of tradition in shipyard families was such that any other career was practically unthinkable. There was no doubt in my mind: I was going to be a 'yard man like my Da' and earn the big money to be had building the massive ships that could often be seen towering over the little back streets of East Belfast.

Ever since the shipyard had opened in 1860 Harland & Wolff had drawn most of its pool of labour from this area, many families having as many as six or seven generations employed 'down the yard'. Having such a close affinity with their workplace inevitably resulted in a sense of isolation and any 'foreigner' such as myself from across the river was viewed with suspicion and not a little distrust. In my early years I would be challenged several times with the remark 'What are you doing here? No jobs to be had on your side of the river then?'

As time went on you would blend into the surroundings and go on to complete your apprenticeship, eventually becoming accepted as 'one of our own'. Unhappily for many, in particular those of a timid disposition, this mockery would prove altogether too much and regrettably a career in shipbuilding would not be for them.

My father had served his apprenticeship as a driller but had then gone on to specialise in the more difficult skill of hole-cutting, not because of the challenge this expertise represented, but simply because it paid an additional trade premium of fifteen shillings a week and he needed the money. Perhaps of more importance, however, having this greater level of skill provided the benefit of making your job more secure when the inevitable lay-offs came, in particular when a vessel was nearing completion. As far back as anyone could remember, Harland & Wolff had maintained the unhappy tradition of making almost all of its newly qualified tradesmen redundant at the end of the week in which they completed their five-year apprenticeship. It was certainly not uncommon for final-year apprentices to find themselves graduating as qualified tradesmen on perhaps a Wednesday, only to suddenly find themselves surplus to requirements and made redundant by the Friday. While this was not an officially sanctioned policy by the company, they nevertheless tacitly approved of this practice, which in itself served to instil in the workforce a very real sense of fear and intimidation. This atmosphere of uncertainty was deliberately created by the management of the company to undermine the self-confidence of the workforce with the specific intention of ensuring that no union, however strong in its organisation, could possibly hope to counteract it. By covertly encouraging and condoning such tactics the company ensured it retained complete control over every aspect of its employees' working lives and made certain any potential troublemakers, such as union activists, were quickly identified and their services rapidly dispensed with.

Finding himself in such a weak position, any newly qualified tradesman, very probably with a wife and young family to provide for, would not be inclined to question or dispute any order or instruction he was given, knowing that the prospects for his continued employment rested almost entirely upon the whim and goodwill of his foreman or line manager. For those fortunate enough to be granted the opportunity of continuing their employment as qualified tradesmen, every facet of the working conditions they would experience, from the manner and nature of the tasks allocated to them to the quality and suitability for purpose of any tools and equipment provided during their service with the company, rested entirely in the hands of individuals who often displayed a sadistic and callous nature to reinforce their almost absolute authority.

Unlike many other similar industries, the Personnel Department in Harland & Wolff, such as it was, played little or no effective part in the selection, discipline or retention of any of its employees. It was the usual established practice in Harland & Wolff that a father or other relation in its current employment would indicate that they wished for their son or nephew etc. to be considered for future employment. In almost every case this request would indeed result in a formal offer of employment being made, usually as a messenger boy to begin with as a precursor to being granted a trade apprenticeship.

On the very rare occasions when an application was made for a female relative, the result would be largely the same, except that in these instances it would generally be clerical or typing positions which would be offered to the applicant. Only in very exceptional circumstances, such as the daughter of a manager or foreman, would an offer of training as a tracer be made. Subsidiary to the various drawing offices throughout Harland & Wolff, the Tracing Department was staffed by an all-female complement of workers who copied or traced the major drawings of each vessel. These drawing copies were reproduced from the paper originals onto a durable linen-based cloth for use onboard the vessel in planning cargo-loading or discharging operations.

In this way the long tradition of generation after generation of family involvement in the company was established and maintained. For anyone outside this exclusive circle the prospects of obtaining employment within Harland & Wolff were remote to say the least. This lax degree of control in regard to the selection and recruitment of its employees only served to further reinforce the almost feudal system of management that existed during these early years, and which inevitably resulted in many cases of injustice and unprofessional conduct among the supervisory management going unpunished.

Not for nothing then did the area outside the central timekeepers' office become known throughout the shipyard as the 'Market Square', where for many years hundreds of men would gather each week hoping to be selected for any work that was available. It was always degrading, and very often heartbreaking, to frequently observe highly skilled men being regarded as little more than cattle awaiting a buyer as they desperately sought to catch the eye of the hiring foreman. All too often these men, desperate for work, found themselves compelled to offer bribes to each of the foremen who were responsible for selecting a group of workers for employment. The most common method was for the bribes to be concealed within match boxes and handed over under the guise of offering a light for a cigarette or pipe. This highly illegal, but nevertheless widespread practice, provided a lucrative sideline for those in a position to take advantage and, depending upon the greed of the official concerned, frequently resulted in more men being taken on than was necessary. So widespread did this scam become that the company was eventually forced, through a combination of embarrassment and threats by some of the victims, to report the matter to the police. In spite of their rather belated attempt to clean up this despicable corruption and punish those involved, the company quickly found that, as was usual on such occasions, those responsible immediately closed ranks, with the result that only one foreman was ever found guilty of corruption and was summarily dismissed.

On the other hand it became widely accepted among the workforce that this miserable individual had been nothing more than a token victim, a scapegoat who found himself sacrificed simply to assuage the guilt the company felt over their complacency in effectively dealing with the racket. Realistically, everyone knew that the main perpetrators of the swindle were too well protected by the wall of silence and intimidation they had built up over the years to be exposed.

Whatever good intentions the company may have had in at last endeavouring to stamp out this abuse of power, it would count for very little while its present managerial regime remained unaltered, and in the end very little would actually change to improve the situation until several years later. To further add to this atmosphere of uncertainty, the spectre of seasonal redundancies was also a common hazard to be faced as an employee of Harland & Wolff. These would invariably strike just prior to the July holiday period otherwise known as the 'Twelfth fortnight', and the prospect of your annual holiday being extended for an indefinite period made this an especially dreaded time. However, by far the worst time psychologically was Christmas, with sometimes thousands of men going home to their families with the news that come the New Year they would need to find a new job.

In later years, when applying for my first mortgage, I jokingly advised the Building Society manager that I could only be considered temporarily employed as I worked for Harland & Wolff. He laughed and responded, 'Oh aye very funny, you had me going there for a moment.' While he may have found my comment amusing at the time, little did he realise I wasn't kidding and had meant every word. I suppose it must be something in our psyche but Belfast folk tend to have a rather fatalistic approach to life and the troubles it can bring, and in that respect I am no different from anybody else born and bred in that great city. Consequently I thought, 'Well it's their money that's at risk so I'll let him do the worrying about it, there's no point in two of us getting upset.' Thankfully, as it turned out neither of us had any cause for concern.

However, at this particular moment in time, thoughts of mortgages and buying houses were a long way removed from my mind; such things were far into the future and very much a world away from my reality. Little did I know it then, but that future would turn out to be a life much more fulfilled than I could ever have hoped to imagine. If I had been able to see what the future held my story would have been radically different, but we are nothing if not slaves to our own destiny and fate.

Lulled by the euphoric combination of warmth and drowsiness, I could feel myself slowly drifting back into sleep when I was suddenly jerked wide awake by a thunderous knocking from down below which reverberated throughout the house. As he passed our house on his daily rounds, the lamplighter had given the large brass knocker on the front door several mighty blows as if he was trying to waken the dead. I always imagined that he rather enjoyed this extra-curricular activity as a 'knocker-up', and at two bob per house it proved a lucrative boost to the meagre wage he received from his employer, the rather grandly named 'Belfast Corporation Gas Department'. Behind him the warm glow from the ancient street lamp bathed the damp pavement around its base in a pool of light, illuminating the many puddles of water formed on the uneven granite slabs that made up the pavement. He rested his 'company vehicle', a rusty old bicycle, against the lamp-post while he reached up with a long pole into the lamp itself to shut off the gas to the mantle, watching as it rapidly cooled from white hot to a powdery grey. 'Oul Davy must think we're all deaf,' I remember muttering to myself as I reluctantly struggled up from the small divan bed and found myself suddenly shivering from the unseasonable cold.

As the last shackles of sleep finally fell away, I slowly became aware of the general clatter of activity from the rooms below accompanied by the aroma of hot toast which permeated the air. As usual my mother had busied herself preparing breakfast for the family before getting herself ready for her job in a clothing factory making overalls and boiler-suits. She was a highly skilled dressmaker, but jobs in this profession were few and far between, so she was forced to adapt her skills to the much heavier work of producing industrial garments. 'Are you going to lie there all day?' she called up the stairs, 'Your breakfast is ready and you know your da will go without you if you aren't ready on time.'

Finally breaking free from the lure of my snug little haven, I forced myself off the edge of the bed and on to my feet where the shock of the cold linoleum on my bare flesh jerked me fully awake. Quickly washing and dressing in our tiny bathroom which Dad had constructed from an alcove that was once an airing cupboard on the landing, I rushed down the staircase that led into the small back kitchen where I came face to face with my father. Looking directly at him I nevertheless waited as usual until he spoke in order to gauge the mood he would be in for that day. After what seemed an eternity but was in reality only a few moments, he spoke: 'I hope you are going to show a bit more life about yourself than you usually do. Today is yer first day in the yard, so just you make sure you don't let me down by acting the damn fool.' 'Not bad,' I thought, 'at least he spoke to me, so we're off to a good start.'

My father was a small man in stature, barely five foot six and no more than ten stone soaking wet, but in common with almost all of his generation of shipyard workers he had developed a hard edge to his character. It was a trait that had served him well over the years and which had helped to shield him from the hard and uncompromising world that was Harland & Wolff. Several years later, as we shared one of our rare father/son conversations, he told me of the mixed emotions he felt that day as he prepared, for the first time, to take me down into the shipyard to begin my working life amid the towering gantries. On one hand he was proud that his son was taking his first steps into the 'real' world of employment, but deep in his heart he harboured a lingering fear about how I would cope in the difficult and dangerous environment of shipbuilding.

My father had been at Harland & Wolff all of his working life, joining the company as an apprentice driller at the tender age of fourteen. His career would span almost fifty years, yet ever since his first day it would be fair to say that he had grown to hate it more with every passing year. These were hard men working in a hard industry, where you had to be tough just to survive the daily routine – let alone the weather. It was bitterly cold in winter, leaving hands blue and frost-bitten as men were forced to chip the ice from the machinery they were to use, and blisteringly hot in summer as the steel of the hull surrounding them absorbed the heat of the sun like some sort of infernal oven. Unsurprisingly, under the stress of such conditions simple arguments would frequently and rapidly escalate into fist fights, especially among the apprentices, who were desperate to establish themselves into some sort of hierarchy or pecking order.

I recall my father telling me how he had once been punched in the face and received a black eye for having the temerity to question an instruction. 'Tell yer Ma how ye got that and you'll get another one to match it tomorrow,' he was sharply told by his assailant. Of course there was no question of either sympathy or remorse ever being offered for this assault, and it would have been foolish indeed to have expected any. As a consequence of all this my father had had to become as hard and as tough as his surroundings if he was to survive in such an environment. However even he could never have anticipated just how hard and difficult that daily battle for survival would become. Indeed, as I was about to discover, it was among these tradesmen, or 'journeymen' as they were better known in shipyard jargon, that bullying and intimidation, especially of apprentices, had over the years been developed into something of an art form.

From the corner of the tiny kitchen I could see my mother, Charlotte, gazing wistfully across at my father and probably wondering just how long it would be before all hell broke loose with the inevitable argument. Despite being only fifteen years of age, I had frequently displayed a wilful side to my character and a fierce independence far beyond my tender years. My father had tried his best to discourage me from following him into the shipyard but I would have none of it, and was determined, as usual, to have my own way. In the end, to all intents and purposes he had to simply bow to the inevitable. Many years later, my mother would confide in me that as she continued to wash the breakfast dishes that morning, she had reflected on how quickly the years had flown since she had held me in her arms as a tiny baby. Even from birth I had displayed an independent streak in arriving almost a fortnight overdue, apparently making my entrance into the world whenever it suited me. 'You were a determined wee bugger even then,' she recalled. Smiling to herself she remembered my reaction to the news that my packed lunch, or 'piece' as it was universally known in Belfast, comprised cheese sandwiches. This was indeed my father's favourite but I loathed and detested cheese in any form, and especially as the filling in sandwiches. I had thought when I left school that my days of the ubiquitous cheese sandwiches for lunch were over, and looked forward to something more imaginative. Of course, what I didn't begin to understand or appreciate was that this was all my mother could afford to provide for our packed lunch. In those days the exotic fillings so commonplace today were unavailable, and even if they had been available my mother couldn't have afforded to buy them anyway. Her face changed for a moment as she reminisced: 'Do you remember what you said that morning?' Without waiting for me to do so she continued. 'Cheese eh? Great, just the thing for a working man.' Unfortunately for me, the cheery manner that I had attempted to affect had backfired rather badly and my remark simply sounded both ungrateful and sarcastic. My father had immediately erupted. 'Listen you ungrateful wee brat! Where the hell do you think you are?? What's wrong with cheese? Not good enough for you, is that it? Well if you don't like it you can do without, OK?'

Shocked by my father's outburst, but hurt more by the realisation that I had deeply upset and offended my mother, and in doing so had inadvertently caused yet another scene, I had tried to in vain to apologise. 'Look I'm sorry Mum, that didn't come out the way I meant it to.' But the damage had been done, and the remainder of breakfast time was spent in stony silence. Vivid recollections of that incident sprang to mind as I remembered her staring at me, her face devoid of all expression as in her usual resigned manner she simply nodded her head in acknowledgement of my desperate attempt at an apology. Even as we recalled the events of that first morning I felt a pang of regret about what had happened. With the benefit of hindsight I could see just how difficult things had been for my mother; struggling to keep hearth and home together was difficult enough without having to act as a referee between her husband and only son. Turning to me once again she said, 'Just for a change it would have been nice if either of you had tried to understand how I felt or appreciated the problems I had, it just wasn't fair.'

Indeed life for my mother was not, and never had been, what could reasonably have been considered to be easy. Ever since she had been a little girl she had realised that anything she hoped and aspired to would be solely dependent on the results of her own hard labour and abilities. As a child she had often dreamed of a big house in the countryside, surrounded by wide green fields where the air was fresh and clean, far, far away from the grim city streets she had known all her life.

Belfast had a long-established and well-deserved reputation for being a hard city presenting a grim face to the world, and offering little in the way of comfort to its citizens. That is not to say the city was without humour, in fact the opposite was true, but it was a grim humour born out of desperation from the grinding poverty coupled with a sharp and unique sense of irony that marked out the people of the city as unlike any other. Like a house divided upon itself it was never truly at peace. It was true enough that during the war years a spirit of camaraderie among the population had developed, but even that was restricted in the main to being 'among your own sort'. On the other hand this was Northern Ireland, religious and political tensions were never far from the surface, and regardless of whatever hardships they had shared both sides harboured a deep and abiding distrust of each other. Despite this, my mother often told me that the years during the Second World War had been the happiest of her life; she had enjoyed her youth earning a living manufacturing parachutes and uniforms for the armed forces. Frequently she and her friends would slip small hand-written notes into the uniform pockets, wishing the recipient luck and letting them know that someone back home was thinking of them. While such activity remained strictly against the rules and was deeply frowned upon by the Ministry of Defence, in reality the factory management turned a blind eye to such high jinks. It was simply a bit of harmless fun and without doubt was very good for the morale of the servicemen who found themselves on the front line or in battle. It was during these heady years that Mum found herself accompanying her friends one evening to a local football club dance, and it was there that she met Dad for the first time. Immediately attracted to each other, they shared the first dance together and had remained in each other's company for the rest of the evening. However, when it came to the art of romance my father had several lessons to learn.

Walking along York Street from Seaview football ground, the home of Crusaders F.C., they were lost in conversation and each other until my father noticed they had reached the junction of Royal Avenue. Turning to my mother he asked, 'Where did you say you lived again?' to which she replied, 'Donegal Road,' which was some four miles further away. 'Ah well I'll bid you good night then, and I'll probably see you next week at the dance,' replied my father, and with that he retraced his steps back up York Street to his home in Greenmount Street. Over the years since, my mother has frequently laughed about my father's perceptible lack of romance or his complete failure to grasp the idea of being in any way the gallant gentleman. 'That was just your father's way and I suppose it added to his charm, not that I appreciated it very much at the time mind you.' Hearing my mother recall such stories about the early years in their relationship, I often wondered just how they actually did fall in love and eventually get married, thankfully for my sake they did!

Her thoughts again returning to that first morning, my mother confessed that she thought my father and I would never leave the house together, or at the very least if we did we would not actually be speaking to each other. 'The pair of you fought like cat and dog that morning, I don't know who was the worst; you or your Da'. In any event, some sort of truce must have been established because the pair of us eventually did depart together, turning left down the rain-swept street towards the docks and the broad reaches of the river Lagan. Walking along together, I remember that we exchanged only a few words, despite the fact that, as usual, our argument had been forgotten almost as quickly as it had begun. Each of us were preoccupied with the expected trials and tribulations of the day ahead as we trudged on through the rain towards the dock gates, and the little ferry boat that traversed the river daily to deliver hundreds of men to the giant shipyard.

Truth be told, I was glad of the silence between us, as my throat had become progressively more parched while the churning feeling in the pit of my stomach had rapidly developed into an overwhelming sensation of nausea. 'Please God,' I thought, 'please don't let me be sick, not today of all days.' My legs had begun to shake, and as each trembling step I took brought me ever closer to Harland & Wolff and the start of my working life, I began to wonder if opting for a job in the shipyard had been a good idea after all. As the conflicting emotions whirled within me, excitement at the prospect of all the new, and as yet undiscovered, things I would experience gradually overcame my feelings of doubt and panic. Certainly I was about to embark on a new and exhilarating period in my life. However, my feelings of excitement were tempered with a very real fear of the unknown. Looking across at my father, I was glad and tremendously grateful that he was beside me. Despite my air of bravado I was reassured by his presence and knew that if the going became too tough 'my da' would not be too far away if I needed some moral support. Despite his fervent opposition to my choice of career and his attempts to discourage me, I knew he would secretly keep an eye on my welfare and ensure I did not get too rough a ride.

Most evenings while sitting at home, more often than not doing my school homework under my mother's strict supervision, I had overheard my father's conversations about his life in the shipyard. Stories of the magnificent vessels he had worked on before they left to sail the oceans of the world, coupled with anecdotes about his colleagues and friends, marvellous tales that had filled my childhood years with wonder. On the other hand I also remembered my father leaving the house, all too frequently, to attend the funeral of one or another of his workmates who had been killed under the unfeeling gaze of the slipway cranes. There were terrible and frightening stories of the dirt, danger and privation faced every day by those who chose to make their living as shipbuilders, haunted by the ever-present spectre of death or serious injury as they earned their daily bread. As a child I had never really understood my father's comment that 'Those killed are the lucky ones; at least they have escaped to the other yard.' However, despite my tender years I had enough sense on hearing this not to question my father too closely or ask him to explain how anyone being killed could be considered lucky, or indeed how, if they were dead, they could possibly have gone to work in another shipyard. In spite of my burning curiosity, I had somehow gained enough intelligence to know this was a very sensitive subject with my father, and one best left alone until I could better understand and appreciate the raw emotions such tragic events released.

After what seemed to be a very short walk through the massive wooden gates that guarded the entrance to the harbour complex, I suddenly found myself approaching the periphery of a crowd of men huddled in a tight mass at the end of the quayside. As I drew nearer I could sense something vaguely familiar about this throng of men, something I couldn't quite comprehend, until slowly the realisation began to dawn on me what it was. They all looked the same as each other, not quite clones or mirror images but nonetheless almost identical in their appearance and manner. Suddenly the reason why these men were so recognisable became clear to me, I had seen their image every day for years as I watched my father leave for work. The cloth cap, the navy blue overalls, the ubiquitous hob-nail boots (known as 'shit kickers'), they were all there, each man dressed the same and each with his lunch or 'piece' for that day tucked under his arm. The more affluent carried theirs in a 'piece box' (an old biscuit tin or enamel box), while the rest of them simply relied on the wrapping paper that came with the loaf of bread used to make their sandwiches. Smiling to myself, I acknowledged the fact that I would probably soon become one of the stereotypical shipyard men I saw before me.

However, the smile rapidly faded from my face as I looked more closely at my companions, each had a haunted and careworn expression on their face, the most disconcerting and striking feature being the tired and lifeless eyes that stared dispassionately across the river towards Harland & Wolff. 'You've suddenly gone very quiet,' my father said as we took our place among the crowd waiting for the small ferry that shuttled back and forth across the river. 'I bloody well hope you aren't having second thoughts about starting here because it's too late now.'

'No,' I replied, 'I'm just a bit surprised by how miserable everybody looks, that's all.' Quickly taking a firm hold of my arm my father whispered into my ear, 'Listen son, one thing you will learn quickly down here is that you can always tell a yard man by his face, and as you'll soon find out they have bugger-all to smile about.'

In my youthful innocence I had fondly imagined that working life would simply be an extension of my school days, I would still be learning but would have the added advantage of being paid to do so. As events would eventually prove, this fanciful impression was very far from reality, but for the moment I remained blissfully unconcerned for the future. That was not to say I was unaware of the hard reputation attached to Harland & Wolff from overhearing various conversations between my father and his friends, and I remember thinking to myself they must be exaggerating because nowhere could be that bad. Whatever the truth of the matter, it was far too late now to have any second thoughts about my choice of career; I was here now and would just have to get on with things as best I could. Of one thing I was certain: if I discovered that I had indeed made a mistake in coming to Harland & Wolff, my father was the last person I would tell.

'This the lad then?' came a gruff voice addressing my father, while at the same time managing to totally ignore the object of his enquiry at his side. 'Aye, that's him right enough,' replied my father, adding almost as an afterthought, 'It's his first day.'

'Jesus Christ Tommy have you no bloody sense?' Came the immediate reply: 'Sure that fucking shipyard is no place for a boy!'

Chapter Two

The little ferry boat slowly pitched and rolled its way across the river, with the occasional stream of spray from the bow soaking those unlucky enough to find themselves standing there. The 'oul hands', with the benefit of many years experience, had all congregated towards the stern of the vessel, thus leaving the foolhardy or inexperienced to act as wind and spray breaks as we headed towards the tiny landing stage at the end of the Victoria wharf. Looking up-river I was shocked to see what appeared to be a giant vessel bearing down on our tiny craft. 'Don't worry young 'un,' said a friendly voice, 'It's only the Liverpool boat late again.' Looking round I found myself staring into the face of the man who just a few minutes before had sounded so gruff. 'Meet the Bear son,' said my father, introducing me to a giant of a man. 'Of course to you he is Mr Matthews.' Thrusting a gnarled hand towards me, which closely resembled a huge paw, I could easily see where he got his nickname from. As my hand disappeared into his massive grip I could feel the bones of my hand being compressed as if in a vice. 'Pleased to meet you,' I mumbled, while still managing to keep one eye on the now rapidly advancing ship, though as it turned out my fears were unfounded and we safely negotiated our crossing of the river. In later years I came to realise that the late arrival of the various cross-channel steamers was a very common occurrence and no real cause for alarm. Of course that didn't stop me adopting an air of bravado when confronted with someone making their first river crossing under similar circumstances.

As we bumped alongside the pontoon which acted as the landing stage, the boat suddenly took on an alarming tilt as those anxious to disembark crowded along the rail. The boatman struggled to keep his craft alongside the jetty as the men jumped across the now widening gap. Grabbing my arm and bodily lifting me up and forwards, my father propelled me off the boat and onto the slippery surface of the pontoon. 'You need to be quicker than that son or you'll be in the drink for sure,' he told me. Steadying myself on the wildly rocking platform I asked why the ferry didn't tie up alongside to let the passengers off safely? My enquiry was answered by laughter from my father and his companion. 'He's a lot to learn about this place hasn't he?' said the bear as he headed towards the steeply angled gangway leading upwards to the quay. Just at that moment the arriving Liverpool ferry *Ulster Queen* steamed past, her backwash causing the already rocking pontoon to buck and pitch wildly, accompanied by some ear-splitting and quite frankly terrifying metallic screeching from the pontoon mooring pins. Struggling for dear life to keep my feet, I rapidly ascended the gangway to the safety of the jetty as soon as I could, making a mental note never to set foot on that bloody ferry again. A solemn vow that would be long forgotten by going home time that evening.

As my father and I walked along the wharf towards the rear entrance to the Queens Shipyard, or 'main yard' as it was better known to those who worked there, the rain had resumed with an even greater intensity, soaking into every fibre of our clothes and turning them into a cloying damp mass. As we trudged onward we passed a small frigate, HMS *Resolute*, which had recently arrived for some much-needed repair work. Looking on in amazement as we passed along the side of the vessel, I noticed two sailors, both soaked to the skin, busily scrubbing the *inside* of an already shining dustbin under the watchful eye of what I took to be an officer. Adding to this surreal scene a naval band in full ceremonial regalia, also exposed to the elements, had been assembled at the stern of the frigate. The band was playing martial music as the white ensign was solemnly and ceremonially raised to the top of the ship's Jack staff (or flag pole). Standing rigidly to attention, a shining brass telescope tucked under his arm as he saluted the flag, was an officer whom I assumed to be the captain. His immaculate uniform was bedecked with rows of brightly coloured medal ribbons, while the gold rings on the cuffs of his jacket were matched by the streamers of gold braid falling from his epaulettes.

Perhaps the greatest indication that my assumption was correct was the fact that he alone was standing under the shelter of a canvas awning protecting him from the inclement weather. For the second time in just a matter of minutes I found myself making another promise; from what I had just seen there was no way in hell I was ever going to join the Navy. It is surprising how little incidents like this can have a profound effect; despite so many years having passed since that morning the image is still as bright and clear in my mind as if it happened only yesterday. The whole scenario had appeared to be so illogical and pointless to my impressionable young mind, nevertheless in the coming years I would witness several such apparently pointless exercises and come to well understand the old military adage 'bullshit baffles brains'. Little did I realise at the time just how much 'bullshit' I would discover in Harland & Wolff, and how much the management relied upon it to conceal their all too obvious shortcomings.

A unique and almost feudal system existed within the company which ensured that almost all managerial appointments were made on the basis of the 'old boy' network. Unfortunately, this inevitably resulted in the establishment of a management structure that almost entirely excluded any individual from outside this select group. The predictable consequence of this flawed selection process was the establishment of a management hierarchy that lacked either the experience or ability to recognise future developments in shipbuilding technology, qualities that were necessary to continually move the shipyard forward. In later years, when competition between shipbuilding companies became stronger, and shipyards across the world were facing grave uncertainties in their fight for survival, Harland & Wolff would find itself ill-equipped to meet these kinds of challenges. The decades of neglect and complacency after the halcyon years of the early 1930s, when the order book was brimming over with new contracts and each slipway was continuously occupied, would exact a terrible toll on the future of the company. Ultimately, Harland & Wolff would become a victim of its own success; despite having been rightly acknowledged as the greatest shipbuilder in the world in its heyday, the seeds of destruction were planted in that period of confidence and self-assurance. This confidence degenerated into complacency, a fall which would eventually lead to the ultimate decline of the company and its complete withdrawal from shipbuilding operations in 2004.

As we entered the shipyard gates my father pointed out the central time office, where I was due to report to the Head Timekeeper and undergo the ritual of being allocated your works personnel number and collecting 'yer board'. 'Just keep straight on son until you come to a small building on yer left,' said my father, pointing to an indeterminate spot at the far end of the cobbled road which ran the length of the Queens Shipyard. 'You'll see a big sign saying time office, that's where ye go in and ask for the Earl of Comber, OK then? Well away ye go,' and with that he disappeared into the throng of passing men heading towards the various building sheds and slipways. By now totally confused, I made my way slowly in the general direction my father had indicated. 'Christ,' I thought as I struggled to comprehend just what my father had said. 'The Earl of Comber works in the shipyard, as a timekeeper. God Almighty, things must be hard if royalty is reduced to that.' It was with such thoughts whirling about my head that I suddenly found myself outside a small, single-storey, red brick building bearing the sign 'Time Office'. Unsure if indeed this was the location where I would find the Head Timekeeper, I stopped a passing worker and asked, 'Is this where I can find the Head Timekeeper?' 'You read?' came a grunt in reply, to which I responded in the affirmative. 'Well don't ask fuckin' silly questions then,' came the blunt answer, and with that he was gone.

Standing there in a state of shock at such an abrupt encounter I was unsure about what I should do next, but certainly I would look out for a friendlier face to ask directions. As it turned out my difficulty was resolved by the arrival of a lad not much older than myself. 'First day is it?' he enquired, 'Not to worry, it's all a bit strange at first until you get used to it. Follow me.' Relieved to place myself at his disposal I followed him into the hallway.

Swiftly following my new-found friend into a vast cavern of a room, I found myself before a long, low table at which were seated several men engrossed in conversation. 'You wait there,' said my companion, 'one of these here men will fix you up with yer board and that.' Remembering Dad's instructions I wondered which, if any of them, was the Earl of Comber and if so, how he should be addressed. As I stood there I tried to imagine what this 'board' would look like and what the hell I was supposed to do with it. I had this surreal image of being presented with a large slab of wood, inscribed with my name, which I would be made to forever carry about the shipyard. Eventually, after what seemed an interminable wait, my presence was finally acknowledged by a curt 'Yes?' from one of the seated men during a convenient pause in their conversation.

'I've to report to the Earl of Comber,' I said, adding by way of unnecessary explanation, 'It's my first day.' At this revelation the assembled group burst into fits of raucous laughter. 'Hey John, here's another lamb to the slaughter for you, looking for his lordship no less.' 'It's obvious he's new to the place, looks as thick as shit if you ask me,' said another. 'Fancy thinking a real life earl worked in this dump! Where the hell they find these lads is beyond me,' he said, while blowing a large smoke ring from his foul-smelling cigarette in my general direction. As the laughter echoed about the room, I failed to understand what was so funny about what I had said. Embarrassed, I had made a complete fool of myself. I wanted to open the door and run away Already I had begun to hate Harland & Wolff and the strange new world I found myself in, perhaps staying on at school wouldn't have been such a bad idea after all.

'Ignore them son, it's just them having a laugh at a new boy's expense, there's no harm meant, they forget they were new themselves once.' Looking round I found myself facing a small, ruddy-cheeked man with a kindly smile playing across his face. 'I'm John, welcome to the shipyard,' he said. 'Pleased to meet you too sir,' I replied, shaking his offered hand. 'It's an honour as I've never met a real life earl before.' Hearing this, the laughter broke out at an even greater volume than before. 'Aw son, I'm not really an earl, that's only a nickname, I can see you have a lot to learn about this place.' With that he indicated that I should follow him towards a small alcove located in the opposite corner of the room. As we walked together John explained that he would issue me with my board number and allocate me to a particular department. Unable to contain my curiosity any longer I simply had to ask 'What's a board?' As if in reply, John reached over to his desk and picked up a small, three-inch long by two-inch wide wooden block with a series of six numbers stamped into a recess along the top edge. Tossing it casually into the air towards me he said, 'That's a board son, and it is the most important bit of gear you will ever have in this place.'

He explained that the number it contained would be my unique personnel number, and that each morning, as I arrived for work, I would report to a check office which would be manned by a timekeeper. In exchange for telling him my personnel number I would be handed my board, which I would keep in my possession until returning it to the check office timekeeper at the end of the working day. John explained that the action of 'drawing yer board' in the morning recorded your attendance that morning, while returning it at night confirmed the number of hours you had been in work that day.

More importantly, it was required each Friday as proof of identity when collecting your wages:

> So you see that little bit of wood is the most important thing you'll ever receive while you work down here, without it nobody knows who you are or how long you've worked that week. Lose it and you don't get no wages, simple as that, so mind you take good care of it.

Motioning for me to sit down facing him, he opened a vast ledger that took up almost all of the desk, 'Your number will be 155314 and you'll have it until you either leave the shipyard or die, whichever is the sooner. I don't care which that is, so make sure you write that down in case you forget it.' After carefully taking a note of my number I asked John when these all-important items would be supplied. 'Ach sure, I'll knock them up for ye in a wee while and you can collect them after the meal hour.'

Thankfully I was already aware from my father that the 'meal hour' referred to the lunch break, and was in actual fact no more than thirty minutes in duration. In all my subsequent years in Harland & Wolff, and despite having unparalleled access to the company archives, I never did discover why the lunch break was universally known as the 'meal hour'. I suppose it will just have to remain one of the unsolved mysteries in the annals of Harland & Wolff. His introduction complete and board number duly recorded, John directed my attention towards a surly-looking youth who was seated behind a small desk piled high with packets and envelopes of various sizes. 'Skite the pish there will take you over to the main gatehouse where oul Harry will look after you and sort you out a run. Best of luck kid, and if you're anything like yer da you'll do OK.'

Dismissing me with a vague wave of his hand, he once again returned to the books and ledgers that lay opened in front of him as I turned towards the lad he had indicated. At the same time I must confess to being slightly amused by the lad's nickname, and couldn't help myself wonder just how he had acquired it. As I approached him however, and caught a whiff of the pungent aroma of stale urine that hung in the air all around him like some acrid fog, I very quickly realised he was quite aptly named.

'You new then?' he enquired, accompanied by a prolonged and very noisy sniff. 'You for number 3 gatehouse then? Waitin' to go to yer time then? What trade are ye down for? Yer da work here? What school did ye go to?' These and a hundred other questions were all asked during the short walk from the time office to my appointed location. Despite his apparently intense interest in every aspect of my personal history and ambitions he never paused between his incessant questions, each one punctuated by an accompanying sniff, to allow me to answer any, or indeed to tell him to mind his own business. Thankfully, we soon arrived outside the gatehouse and I was ushered inside to meet the man who would be in charge of me for the next twelve months, until I became old enough at sixteen to commence my apprenticeship. Pushing me inside, Skite the pish hissed into my ear, 'I'm not allowed in there. I don't think that oul get likes me, he keeps telling me to fuck off.' Desperately holding my breath at his close proximity, it wasn't hard to understand why. 'This is a new lad for ye,' he announced rather unnecessarily, and with a final push propelling me into the room he was gone.

Looking about me I found myself standing before a long, semi-circular counter about four feet in height, behind which stood a rather portly figure. The room itself was about twenty foot square with a high vaulted ceiling stained yellow from years of cigarette smoke.

Along one wall stood a low, bench-type cupboard upon which three lads about my own age were seated; one was reading a rather dog-eared copy of the *Victor* boys magazine, while the other two were engaged in a furious game of shove ha'penny along the seat between them. 'I've been expecting you. Hopefully you don't stink like that other wee shite, took months to get rid of the smell when I threw him out.' With that he thrust his hand towards me, 'The name's Harry, what's yours?'

Taking the offered hand I mumbled 'Thomas', to which he abruptly responded, 'Ah well that'll be Tommy while you work down here. The only Thomas ever to be known in the history of the shipyard was the great Thomas Andrews, and you aren't him are ya?', adding by way of explanation, 'More's the pity as we could do with a few more like him around here.'

At the time I hadn't a clue who Thomas Andrews was, or indeed that he had been the designer of probably the most famous ship in the world, the *Titanic*, but as events would later turn out our paths would become intertwined to an amazing extent. 'That's fine by me, err Harry,' I muttered, 'pleased to meet you too, and no I don't stink, well at least I hope I don't.' 'Well said son!' Harry laughed, 'Welcome to my little empire. Hang yer coat up in that there yonder cupboard and I'll introduce you to these gobshites who'll be yer mates and look after you until you find yer feet.' Turning his attention towards the two lads engrossed in their game he bellowed, 'If you pair don't quit playing that bloody game for five minutes I'll shove that board up your arses so help me God I will!'

Unfortunately his dire threat appeared to have very little impact upon the tournament in progress, with the result that he was compelled to attract their attention by marching across the room and physically grabbing each one by the scruff of the neck and yanking them to their feet. The coins, that just a few moments before had represented the football team of the day, pinged off the wall as they scattered in all directions, some disappearing forever behind a large panelled radiator that dominated one side of the room. Still maintaining his grip on each boy, Harry nodded in my general direction while yelling directly into their faces, 'This here is the new lad Tommy, he'll be doing the main yard run, so you two wee shites take him out and show him the route, NOW!' The last word arrived like a clap of thunder, coinciding as it did with him releasing his grip on the now struggling bodies as he opened the door. From past experience both lads obviously knew what was about to follow as each one made a weaving dart for the entrance, swiftly followed by a boot up the backside to encourage them on their way. 'Well what are you still standing there for?' Harry bellowed, 'Waitin' for somebody to carry you? Get out there with those two and don't come back for at least an hour.'

My companions introduced themselves as Jim and Dundrum, actually the latter's name turned out to be Arnold, but as he hailed from a small County Down fishing village he was, in shipyard logic, forever to be known as Dundrum. However, Arnold would go on to obtain fame and notoriety for quite another reason a few months later. During the quiet spells between the deliveries of mail and the like that each message boy undertook, we usually assembled in the gatehouse for our fast and furious shove ha'penny matches. We were strictly forbidden to go behind the counter into Harry's inner sanctum; to be caught doing so resulted in a swift smack across the head followed by the ubiquitous boot in the arse as you were ejected back to your side of the counter. The day all hell broke loose started like any other, except that, unbeknown to us, this day coincided with a large delivery of money to the cashier's office directly opposite the gatehouse.

Harry had been called away for a while and so Arnold, ever the nosy bugger, took the opportunity to have a root about in the various drawers and cupboards Harry had on his side of the counter. During his exploration he discovered a mysterious button hidden away from view under the edge of the counter top, which he of course pressed. Nothing happened, or so he thought, so he pressed it again a few more times just to be sure – still nothing – so he carried on his investigations into the various cupboards and drawers. He had just returned to our side of the counter as Harry returned to the gatehouse, blissfully unaware of the bedlam that was about to break-out all around us. Suddenly the air was filled with the sound of screeching brakes, as several police vehicles converged on the area with sirens blaring and blue lights flashing. Policemen, several armed to the teeth and all carrying drawn batons, charged into the cashier's office entrance, pushing and shoving each other in their eagerness to get inside. We of course, watching from the other side of the courtyard, were thrilled by the unfolding drama; regrettably Harry had another view on the frantic commotion taking place before his horrified gaze.

As he stood there, all colour visibly drained from his face, he gripped the edge of his chair for support as his knees slowly buckled under him. In our excited chatter none of us had noticed that Harry had gone unusually quiet, given all the activity going on just outside, that was until we noticed him slumped on his chair like some lifeless rag doll.

'What's up Harry?' somebody asked, 'You not well or something? Yer missing all the action out here.' Now visibly shaking, he rose unsteadily to his feet, his face ashen and hands trembling. 'Were any of youse lot behind this counter and did youse touch ANYTHING!?' The last word exploding from his mouth almost as a scream, each of us looked at each other not daring to speak, well aware from Harry's startling reaction that something terrible had happened. After what felt an eternity, Arnold hesitatingly came forward. 'I was, Harry, but the button didn't do anything, I just pressed it but honestly nothing happened, I just pressed it a few times.' Arnold's voice faded off to a whisper as he watched Harry's face change from deathly white to crimson, in the blink of an eye he suddenly made a lunge for Arnold, who, luckily for him, was safely out of reach. Realising he was obviously in deep trouble but unsure why, he opted for discretion rather than valour and bolted out the door.

'Aw, fuck me pink, I don't believe it,' groaned Harry, slapping his hand to his forehead. 'Get the fuck out of here the lot of ye, and if any of you find that big stupid cunt out there throw him in the tide before I murder him.'

We later discovered that Arnold had activated a silent alarm designed to alert the harbour and civilian police to a possible robbery taking place in the cashier's office. These authorities were always advised by Harland & Wolff when large cash shipments were to be received, and they were therefore on high alert for any attempted robbery. The activation of the silent alarm had brought the swift arrival of a number of armed response units, who were not best pleased to discover the whole thing had been a false alarm.

Unfortunately, as a result of the false alarm, Harry found himself on the carpet before the company secretary, who had had to use all of his considerable diplomatic skills to smooth over the whole incident. Obviously it was a serious matter, and the repercussions for the company could have been severe and far-reaching in terms of security. Much oil had to be poured upon the troubled waters, and that Christmas an unusually generous donation of corporate gifts was made to the officials who had cooperated in burying the whole incident far away from any official report. We message boys, on the other hand, were not quite so fortunate, and experienced a harsh reaction from Arnold's catastrophic adventure with the silent alarm. From that day on we found ourselves banished from the warmth of the gatehouse to a small and damp lobby opposite, where we were to remain under strict supervision. Gone forever were the shove ha'penny tournaments and the opportunity to warm our bums along the radiator on cold winter days. However, things were considerably worse for Arnold, as he found himself banished to the roughest and most inhospitable part of the shipyard, officially known as the 'Thompson Triangle', or more commonly simply as 'deep water'.

The 'Thompson Triangle' had a fearsome reputation among those who found themselves working there. In winter the rains felt as if they had arrived direct from the Arctic and sliced your skin to the bone, while the fierce wind that constantly blew in from Belfast Lough was known as the 'lazy wind' because it would go through you rather than around you. Arnold lasted a mere five months there before he conceded defeat and handed in his resignation. After a few weeks Arnold and his high jinks had been forgotten. However, the day the 'peelers' came would become part of shipyard legend.

The cashier's office did have another unfortunate claim to fame some months later in an episode that would tax the Inland Revenue to the limit of its patience, and yet, like most instances of disaster, it all began with the best of intentions. As the message boys approached their sixteenth birthday they were required to undergo an aptitude test to determine which trade, if any, they were best suited to. Anyone not reaching the minimum standard for their preferred trade was offered an alternative. However, all this depended on first passing a strict medical examination conducted by the company medical officer. Occasionally someone would fail to reach the necessary medical standard and would therefore be unable to undertake an apprenticeship. However, in such cases a clerical job would be found for the unfortunate individual. While doubtless disappointed at being rejected to learn a trade, at least they still had a job and some prospect of a career.

Just such an individual was Archie, a tall, thin rake of a boy who always displayed a sickly complexion and a hacking cough which was exacerbated by the Woodbines that dangled incessantly from his nicotine-stained lips. Not that any of this bothered him, as he frequently boasted he could hack and spit farther than any of us could, and anyway the cough helped him see better by making his eyes water. It was not a great surprise when we learnt that Archie had failed his medical examination and wouldn't be joining us as the class of '66 in the training centre.

Archie was destined for a career in the cashier's office as a junior clerk, although none of us at the time could have anticipated just how brief a career this would turn out to be. In any event, come his sixteenth birthday Archie duly reported to the Finance Department and was allocated a desk at the rear of the cashier's general office. By way of a gentle introduction to his new role, Archie was given the task of inputting the new tax codes that had arrived from the Inland Revenue for each employee. Many codes had not changed, but each one still had to be manually cross-checked and amended as necessary; unfortunately this simple task would end in unmitigated disaster, as nobody had realised that Archie couldn't read or write.

To further complicate matters, Archie had knocked the large file containing the individual coding notices onto the floor, with the result that the alphabetically arranged documents were now in a complete jumble. Horrified at what had befallen him, Archie swiftly gathered together the wayward papers and manfully tried to carry on, hoping against all hope that no harm had been done. Quite why Archie had hoped the coding notices would have somehow rearranged themselves back into the correct order was never explained, suffice to say Sod's Law took over and the situation was about to get very much worse. Remorselessly pressing on with his task, Archie did his best to compare each name on the notices with those on the printed payroll sheets before him. Using the simple expedient that if symbols looked the same on each document they were correct, he carefully amended any figures that looked different on the notices from those on the payroll sheets.

Sadly, his good intentions had only succeeded in completely upsetting thousands of tax codes and causing devastation to the payroll system. Married men with several children suddenly found themselves being taxed as single men, while conversely single men suddenly found themselves unexpectedly wealthy as their tax deduction virtually disappeared. Unfortunately for Archie, the storm didn't break until the first pay day of the new tax year, unfortunate as, in an effort to cover his tracks, Archie had systematically destroyed all the coding notices, thus compounding the confusion. As the storm raged around him Archie did his best to placate the head cashier, who struggled to understand just how such a disaster could have happened. 'How the hell did you do it?' demanded his boss, 'Can't you bloody read?', to which of course Archie meekly replied 'No.'

The chaos took almost three months to sort out and meant the employment of a full-time contingent from the Inland Revenue of an Inspector and four senior officers, together with almost all the Harland & Wolff Payroll Department. Not that this was of any interest or concern to Archie, his employment having been terminated some time previously.

As I became more familiar with my surroundings I quickly settled into a comfortable routine and began to recognise the various departments by their normal abbreviated designations. For example N.D.O. was recognised as the Naval Drawing Office, while the Contracts and Buying Department simply became known as C.&B. However, despite my new-found ability to interpret such colloquial names, I continued to stumble over my recognition of what was an actual name rather than a nickname of the individual yard managers and foremen; this inability to differentiate would inevitably lead to disaster.

I had been given a roll of urgent drawings to deliver to the Queens Shipyard, with instructions that they were without fail to be handed directly to the head foreman caulker. As I marched across the yard I suddenly realised I did not know the name of the person I was instructed to find and so asked a passing worker for some assistance. 'Excuse me,' I said politely, 'I'm looking for the head foreman caulker but I don't know his name or where his office is, can you help me?' 'No problem son, it's old Ironhead you want and his hut is over yonder behind the platers' shed,' he replied, indicating the direction I needed to go. Following his instructions I duly arrived outside a large wooden hut, knocked on the door and went in. 'Excuse me Mr Ironhead,' I said, 'I have some urgent drawings for you.'

His face suddenly went bright crimson. 'What did you call me boy?' he thundered, 'You cheeky wee bugger, I'll kick your arse for ye.' As I stood there, completely amazed at his reaction, I couldn't understand for the life of me what I'd said or done to annoy him. 'Go on, clear-off and don't come back!' he shouted, as I backed out of the hut and closed the door. Returning to my base in the main gatehouse, hurt and confused by what had happened, I decided to tell Harry all about it and hopefully get some sort of explanation as to what I had done wrong. As I related my tale of woe he suddenly burst out laughing, 'Mr Ironhead you called him? No bloody wonder he went mad, his name is McCauley.'

Harry went on to explain that Charlie McCauley was a well-known amateur footballer who played for the local side Crusaders. He had a reputation as a formidable header of the ball and as such had acquired the nickname 'Ironhead'. 'Don't worry about it son, I'll speak to him and clear everything up,' Harry laughed and, true to his word, he telephoned Charlie McCauley and explained just what had happened. A few days later, as chance would have it, I had another delivery of drawings for 'Ironhead', only this time I made sure I addressed him properly as Mr McCauley.

Chapter Three

Of course life in Harland & Wolff was not always so amusing; the work was often dirty and dangerous, with little or no regard given to the provision of a safe working environment for the employees. Until the introduction in the 1980s of stringent Government regulations on Health and Safety, which compelled the company to drastically review its procedures, death and serious injury in the steelworking trades was a common occurrence. On average, each vessel under construction would claim two lives and probably account for the maiming of up to ten more. The loss of fingers or toes was regarded as an occupational hazard, more to be endured as the price of the job rather than because of any lack of safety equipment or facilities. Often such injuries gave rise to a unique brand of black humour; employees who had injured a foot or leg, resulting in a permanent limp, were inevitably christened 'Nail in the Boot', likewise anyone suffering the loss of a hand or arm became forever known as 'One Wing'.

Harland & Wolff were by no means benevolent in the face of such injuries, and any employee taking action against the company for compensation for industrial injuries very quickly found themselves ostracised and without a job. Furthermore, using the old boy network that flourished between the engineering employers throughout Northern Ireland, word rapidly spread that here was a trouble-maker and someone who could not be trusted or relied upon. As a consequence of this malicious gossip, these unfortunate individuals found it virtually impossible to obtain regular or full-time employment in the engineering industry, and found themselves having to accept menial and low-paid jobs in order to support their families. Certainly they had a choice: sue Harland & Wolff, who would fight them every step of the way, for compensation for their injury, or keep their mouth shut and be kept on the payroll. While this was no guarantee of permanent employment, it was generally accepted that in return for not causing the company any embarrassment or difficulty a job of some description would be found for them, at least until they had recovered sufficiently to seek alternative employment elsewhere. Unfortunately, it is a hard fact of life that there is no sentiment in shipbuilding, and Harland & Wolff had always made it abundantly clear to any disabled employee that they had no long-term use for those whom they regarded as being crippled. This insulting and derogatory term was frequently used to describe employees who had become disabled to some degree, despite the fact that it was Harland & Wolff, with their blatant lack of regard for the safety and welfare of their employees, who were probably responsible for them being injured in the first place. Unquestionably this practice of discrimination against the less able-bodied was completely immoral, but at the time it was nonetheless quite within the law. Still, the company was careful to keep such activities a closely guarded secret, and would always vigorously reject any suggestion that its employment practices were anything less than fair and equitable. For those unfortunate enough to have suffered a debilitating injury in the course of their duties, the truth of the situation was very different indeed.

Given the advances in legislation governing the safety and welfare of employees, it is difficult today to comprehend the working practices and conditions that existed throughout the yard in those years, and the degree of tolerance and acceptance they enjoyed. On several occasions men lost their lives simply because of the crass indifference, bordering on stupidity, of their overseers, who frequently regarded those under their control as little more than an expendable commodity. Under the archaic, almost feudal system that prevailed during that time, the foreman in charge held complete sway over every aspect of their employees' working lives. With frightening regularity men were ordered to carry out potentially dangerous operations without adequate safety precautions being put in place, or without provision of the proper equipment necessary to complete the task in a safe and sound manner. On several occasion this reckless disregard for human life resulted in disastrous consequences, and it is no surprise to learn that on average two men were killed per vessel under construction. While death and serious injury were commonplace, such incidents were nevertheless still a horrifying experience for those who witnessed them. Even today, several years on, I can vividly recall my father returning home one evening white and shaking with shock at an incident he had observed that afternoon.

The day had been particularly windy, with strong to gale force gusts blowing up the exposed foreshore of Belfast Lough. It was in these difficult conditions that a foreman had ordered the lifting of a large section of bulkhead from the quayside onto a vessel undergoing construction. Under normal circumstances the prevailing wind speed at that time would have meant that such an operation would have been judged unsafe to carry out, and the lift would have been postponed until better weather conditions or a much larger squad of men were available. Extra men would provide additional stability to the section by means of extra guy ropes as the lift commenced. Regardless of the obvious danger and the potential hazard to the life and limb of those engaged on such an operation, the decision whether to proceed or not was entirely at the discretion of the foreman concerned. Furthermore, the company placed absolutely no requirement upon him to consult with any of his superiors on whether to undertake such a hazardous operation in the prevailing conditions, or to seek further advice or assistance regarding a risk assessment before commencing operations. In short, the foremen were empowered with complete discretion over all aspects of their particular areas, even though the vast majority did not possess the necessary training to oversee all aspects of the tasks under their operational control. While each foreman was highly skilled in his particular trade and possessed a working knowledge of shipbuilding generally, it was illogical to expect him to also possess the additional knowledge to understand or appreciate the particular nuances associated with every operation he could be called upon to oversee. This lack of formal training in the recognition and assessment of hazardous operations was nothing less than a recipe for disaster, as it would again prove to be on this particular day.

The wind, which had been gusting strongly all morning, appeared to have increased in velocity as the large flat-steel panel was hoisted into the air. The swirling wind caused the bulkhead section to swing and buck wildly as it dangled precariously from the end of the lifting hook on the crane.

The crane cables groaned and creaked ominously as they became increasingly strained under the stresses imposed on them. The section twisted violently in the air, causing the crane jib to rock wildly from side to side, allowing clouds of rust particles to waft into the air, temporarily blinding those below with a fine red mist of dust. In an effort to reduce this severe motion, two men were delegated to attach ropes to the bulkhead in order to stabilise and reduce the amount of swinging caused by the strong wind. Manfully they struggled to accomplish this, all the while being pulled almost off their feet as the bulkhead was lifted higher into the air, until it was finally in position above the vessel. To precisely lower such a massive structure into a confined space, even in calm conditions, took a tremendous amount of skill and coordination; to attempt such an operation in such blustery condition was highly dangeous, and displayed a callous disregard for even the most basic safety considerations.

As the bulkhead continued to swing high above the open space on the vessel, the two men were instructed to descend into the hold and guide the bulkhead into its final position, using the ropes they had attached earlier. To aid this process they were also provided with a pinch or crowbars, which were used to finally move the bulkhead into position by inserting the bars through pre-drilled holes in the bulkhead and ship structure. This action would allow other men to insert bolts through additional locating holes, thus securing the bulkhead in place prior to final riveting or welding. Everything appeared to be going well as the bulkhead was slowly lowered into place, until it was suddenly struck by an especially strong gust of wind which caused it to violently lurch to the left. The suddenness of the movement took the two men completely by surprise and yanked the ropes controlling the bulkhead out of their hands, with the result that, now free of any restraint, it slammed into the two hapless men, crushing them against the side of the hold.

Such was the severity of the impact that neither man had any chance of survival, their bodies reduced to little more than a bloody pulp beyond human recognition. The bulkhead which had caused the carnage was quickly lowered down to the deck where it would remain until a squad of men could be found to clean up the bloody remains and hose-down the affected area. Despite the horrific nature of such an incident, it was not unusual in such circumstances for any incriminating evidence to be 'accidentally' removed or destroyed in order to conceal the actual sequence of events prior to the arrival of the accident investigators. A bad safety record, or poorly maintained equipment documentation, would result in the company being forced to pay substantial insurance premiums for employee and public liability insurance cover. Accordingly everything possible would be done to avoid giving a poor impression of company safety standards.

So complete was the level of disregard for employee welfare and safety, it had become custom and practice for the true circumstances surrounding any serious accident to be covered-up. This was especially common in the case of an accident involving scaffolding, or 'staging' as it is better known in shipbuilding operations.

The 'staging' surrounding the hull of a vessel usually comprised of wooden, or in later years metal, upright supports with plank walkways laid at various levels around the hull under construction. Often these planks would be in a very poor condition due to their age and constant exposure to the elements, the constant cycle of being soaked by rain and snow resulting in their being warped and therefore unstable when walked on. This tendency to rock from side to side without warning was a particular danger when the planks were wet and/or coated in bird droppings. These droppings were a particular nuisance in the mornings, as they built up to a thick film overnight from the vast flocks of starlings that roosted in the steelwork of the cranes and staging itself. Over the course of a weekend, especially if no overtime was being worked, these droppings could accumulate to a coating almost half an inch thick and had the consistency of grease. Consequently, the combination of rain over the weekend and copious amounts of bird droppings made the surface of the staging planks something akin to a skating rink. Factor in the additional hazard of warped planking, and the potential for disaster became all too obvious, and sure enough disaster there would be.

It had been a particularly cold mid-November weekend, with frequent showers of sleet and snow causing the temperature to hover continually around freezing. That Monday morning, as the men crunched their way through the icy patches that littered the ground all across the Queens Shipyard, they could see the hull of *La Estancia*, a bulk carrier under construction for Buries Marks Ltd, glistening in the half-light of dawn as the weak rays of the sun caused the frost covering it to twinkle like a million stars. Carefully climbing the staging, the more experienced among them used their boots to scrape the frozen coating of bird droppings and ice away from their workplace. Any attempt to operate machinery, usually weighing upwards of thirty pounds, without the benefit of a secure footing, was simply asking for trouble. No matter how careful you might be, the unexpected was invariably on hand to trap the unwary.

In this particular incident a riveter burdened with the weight of his riveting machine, together with several lengths of air hose, attempted to move along the staging to his appointed workplace on the ship. In the half-light and over-burdened as he was, he failed to notice that one of the staging planks he was about to step onto was warped. That was until the moment he stepped on it and was suddenly thrown violently off-balance. As his feet skidded from beneath him he desperately struggled to regain his balance on the slippery surface, however the combination of his sudden movement, the violent rocking of the plank and the icy surface all caused him to be pitched forwards and sideways off the staging. Still forlornly clutching the heavy equipment, his body performed a slow pirouette through the air as he plunged earthwards until, after what seemed an eternity to those of us watching this macabre scenario, eventually smashing into the concrete slipway with a sickening thud that was clearly heard across the entire slipway. Milliseconds after he had struck the ground his machinery crashed down on top of him, crushing what little chance he had of survival after the fall.

Once again the construction of a vessel had needlessly claimed a life, and once again the inevitable cover-up began. Various managers and foremen arrived from their warm offices to inspect the scene of the tragedy, and very quickly they discovered the warped staging plank. Orders were immediately issued to obtain a replacement plank, which was quickly put in place while the dangerous one was swiftly removed and spirited away to be burnt, thus obliterating all evidence of dangerous equipment. Missing or broken handrails were also replaced, while squads of labourers were tasked to quickly remove all traces of ice or bird droppings, together with spreading sand along the staging walkways to ensure adequate grip underfoot. The usual photographs taken by the accident investigators of the scene, which would be used later at the inquest into the tragedy, therefore presented an impression of a safe working environment fully in accordance with, or even exceeding, the requirements of Government safety legislation.

The tragedy would therefore be seen as another unfortunate accident, with little or no blame being attached to Harland & Wolff. As a consequence, the widow and family of the unlucky victim would receive only the minimum award of compensation for their loss and suffering, while unbeknown to them also helping to protect the reputation of Harland & Wolff as a caring and responsible employer. Even more important from the company's point of view, they avoided incurring a drastic increase in their employer's liability insurance premium or being forced to face a wholesale investigation into their employment practices. The provision of employee and public liability insurance had always been regarded by the directors as an unnecessary evil, more of an administrative irritation which was nothing more than a wasteful drain on company finances rather than a useful benefit.

In addition to these underhand and devious methods, those who had witnessed the events of that morning were left in no doubt as to what the consequences would be for them personally should they choose to cooperate with the accident investigators. These investigators were appointed by the insurance company, and along with the factories inspectorate had responsibility for establishing the truth. While no direct or attributable threat to their continued employment was ever officially made by the company or its managers to any of its employees, it was nevertheless made abundantly clear, by means of veiled warnings and intimidation, that anyone attempting to speak out would be considered to be indulging in a severe breach of trust and so quickly find themselves without a job. Additional pressure to remain silent came from the knowledge of the power and outreach the company had established within the wider business community and Government. Any employee who fell foul of this unspoken code of silence would quickly find themselves unfairly branded as a troublemaker and subsequently blacklisted, making the search for another job virtually impossible. They would also find that any welfare benefits to which they or their family were entitled would be inexplicably delayed. A further 'punishment' inflicted on such hapless individuals would be to find themselves offered totally unsuitable jobs which, had they refused to accept, would have resulted in their claim for unemployment benefit being rejected, thus imposing even further hardship on the unfortunate victim.

Another quite subtle and devious twist to this campaign of intimidation relied upon the DSS regulation which stipulated that the first three days of any period of unemployment did not count for benefit purposes. The wretched former employee would find themselves being recalled for employment by the company midway through their first week of unemployment, thus losing their entitlement to benefit for that week. Upon return to the company they would be allocated the worst and most dangerous tasks until they found themselves dismissed once again, usually after a few weeks, when the whole malicious cycle would begin all over again. In utilising such vindictive methods the company engendered an atmosphere of fear and total control over its workforce, both through intimidation and the demonstration of dire consequences for any employee who had the audacity to challenge its authority.

Of course, not all accidents had fatal consequences or took place exclusively aboard vessels under construction; many occurred when repair work was being carried out to vessels in dry-dock or in port, which by the very nature of the tasks involved meant additional safety hazards. When undertaking such work, the shipyard is always keen to maximise its potential profit, while the ship owner, on the other hand, is determined to keep his costs and the vessel's time in dock to a minimum. This conflict of interests can, and usually did, result in dangerous situations being allowed to develop, mainly due to the continual pressure being applied by both Harland & Wolff and the vessel owner to complete the repairs to the vessel as quickly as possible. The inevitable consequence of such haste was an almost complete disregard for the safety of those working aboard the vessel.

Just such a situation may best be illustrated by the following example, which took place in December 1958 aboard the *Esso Glasgow*, an oil tanker undergoing repairs in the Thompson dry-dock.

It had been announced that afternoon that the vessel was scheduled to leave Belfast on the next high tide that evening, and in preparation for this departure the re-flooding of the dry-dock would commence in a few hours time. This decision resulted in frantic efforts by those working on the dock floor and underneath the vessel to complete their tasks so they could move their tools and equipment up onto the dockside. Such was the haste to complete the remaining work on the hull before the scheduled flooding operations that several men had been redeployed to the dock floor from their previous duties. Unfortunately, this had the effect of leaving the tasks they were previously engaged on in an unknown, and therefore potentially unsafe, condition. One of the tasks left unfinished was the re-installation of a major water main along the upper deck of the vessel. This water main comprised of a series of twenty-four-inch-diameter pipes, which, when bolted together through a system of flanges, carried sea water, under enormous pressure, the entire length of the vessel. During the course of the repair work this pipeline had been completely renewed, and had been in the process of being finally bolted together when the fitters involved had been called away, leaving the work incomplete. This had resulted in some pipe flanges only being connected to the next one by means of a few bolts rather than the usual thirty-six. However, to the casual observer nothing would have appeared amiss.

Several hours later the dock had been fully re-flooded, with the vessel now afloat in almost thirty feet of water, held steady and in place by a few ropes secured to bollards on the dockside. A few men could be seen balanced precariously on a small section of staging which hung over the side of the vessel. Busily engaged in drilling the last few holes necessary to install a minor item of equipment, they were blissfully unaware of the drama about to unfold above them. Without bothering to physically check the work had been completed, and assessing the situation by no more than a casual glance at the pipeline, a shipyard manager had issued instructions for the newly installed water main to be fully pressurised prior to testing. This water main, under normal operating conditions, has an internal pressure of 1,200lbs per square inch. However, on this occasion it would thankfully not reach such an enormous pressure. As the pumps forced water down the pipe, the internal pressure climbed steadily until it was estimated it reached just over 700lbs per square inch before the inevitable occurred. With a shattering bang akin to a bomb exploding, the pipeline broke apart at the unsecured flange, sending a torrent of water cascading across the deck and onto the men clinging to the staging below, washing them off the platform and into the dank and freezing waters of the now flooded dry-dock.

Still clutching the heavy machinery he had been using a moment before, one of the drillers plunged into the icy water and straight down to the bottom of the dock some forty feet below. Struggling to regain his feet on the slippery concrete, his lungs struggling desperately with the effort of holding his breath as he fought to control the panic and terror that was engulfing him, he desperately groped in the darkness under the water, until his hands found the stepped sides of the dry-dock and he gratefully pulled himself upwards as fast as he could. Just as he felt his lungs would explode, his head burst out from under the water into the life-giving air. Clinging to the side of the dock steps, his body trembling uncontrollably from the effects of shock, he gulped down great breaths of cold air which made him cough and splutter as it filled his aching lungs. Grateful to have survived such a terrifying ordeal, he lay alongside the freezing concrete of the dockside desperately gripping the unyielding surface with every ounce of whatever strength he still possessed. As he lay there, frantically panting to regain some sort of equilibrium to his senses, he became aware of a babble of voices and bodies surrounding him, however his mind, still in turmoil from the events of the past few minutes, simply refused to comprehend or acknowledge their presence.

Slowly the babble of voices began to make sense in his head as comprehension slowly returned. 'For fucks sake get him up out of there.' 'Christ, is he still alive?' 'Get his boots off.' 'Get a rope round him in case he falls back in.' 'C'mon Tommy, get yer arse up here now, cause if you fall back in there don't think I'm goin' in after you.'

Among all the clamouring voices that last one brought a welcome return to reality – it was none other than the familiar voice of his long-time friend and colleague 'Wee Billy'. Aware that he had to make the effort to move, but still unable to control the violent trembling in his arms and legs, he was forced to crawl on hands and knees towards the top, reassured by the number of willing hands reaching out and taking a firm grip of his sodden clothing.

With a superhuman effort he finally managed to reach the top of the dockside, where he found himself confronted by his foreman, who eyed him rather quizzically and then asked, somewhat pointlessly, 'Are you all right after your little swim?' To work in Harland & Wolff is to understand that such a remark is not intended to be funny, rather it serves as a release from the tension of the moment, a way of coping with a narrow escape from almost certain death and the hazards faced every day. 'You'd better get yourself home and into some dry clothes. I'll give you a pass-out to cover your absence until you come back,' continued the foreman, reaching into his pocket for the book of pass-out dockets. These 'pass-out' dockets had to be obtained to authorise the absence from the company premises of any employee at any time during working hours; the discovery of any unauthorised absence would usually result in instant dismissal. These pass-outs would be presented to the individual's timekeeper, who would note the exact time of exit; upon their return the employee would again report to the timekeeper, who noted the time of their return and length of absence on the pass-out docket. These details would also be recorded in the employee's time book, and the completed pass-out would be returned by the employee to his respective foreman who, in due course, would use the pass-out to check against the time book record.

As a company, Harland & Wolff displayed very little interest in the general welfare of its workers, and actively discouraged any of its employees from requesting time off work to conduct urgent personal business, including medical or hospital appointments. Any and all absences from company premises were to be accounted for to the minute, and all absences, apart from in exceptional circumstances, would be at the employee's expense. Astonishingly enough, it would appear that being washed into a flooded dock and almost drowning was not considered by the company to be an exceptional circumstance, as my father would discover when he received his wages the following Friday (for it was indeed he who had almost drowned that freezing December day). Receiving his payslip that Friday afternoon, my father was astounded to note that a deduction of two hour's pay had been made from his wages to cover the time taken by him to return home and change into some dry clothes. His subsequent protests at the unfairness of such harsh treatment, particularly as he was not to blame for his enforced absence and had actually had to be sent home by his foreman, were bluntly swept aside with the reminder that he was lucky to have survived and therefore to still have a job.

Such incidents were typical of the prevailing working conditions within Harland & Wolff at the time. However, conditions did slowly improve, as later Governments introduced legislation designed to improve Health and Safety within the workplace. While Harland & Wolff were by no means unique in such treatment of their employees, and indeed their uncaring attitude towards their workforce could be said to be fairly typical of British shipyards, they were perhaps among the harshest. Since the days when Edward Harland had sacked the entire workforce, the company management had adopted a policy of using fear and intimidation to control its employees.

Unions were effectively banned for several years, and anyone found to be encouraging such activity very quickly found himself without a job or any prospect of gaining one elsewhere in Northern Ireland. Such was the power and outreach of Harland & Wolff that anyone it considered undesirable became virtually unemployable as word of his transgression was passed to other prospective employers. As the largest employer in the country, Harland & Wolff enjoyed the luxury of virtual autonomy in its actions. It could afford to impose its will – no matter how unreasonable that may have been – upon its employees, without any fear of industrial action or censure. The result was a browbeaten and increasingly disgruntled workforce, forced to endure often draconian conditions while labouring in an atmosphere of paranoia and distrust. These hapless individuals were trapped by circumstances far beyond their control, and the simple necessity of retaining their employment far outweighed any desire to challenge the company on its working practices, especially given the inevitable outcome of such folly.

In its later years the company would find itself faced with many thousands of claims for industrial injuries, caused in the main by their failure to provide proper safety equipment or training for those charged with the supervision of employees. Such was the financial impact of agreeing a settlement figure in each of these claims, the company's principal insurer found itself facing a financial crisis from which they never recovered, and as a result they were forced to withdraw from providing any further insurance cover. Today, under the strict conditions laid down by statute covering an employer's responsibility to provide a safe working environment for their employees, and the provision of adequate insurance cover, such scandalous practices would be impossible for any employer to even contemplate, let alone get away with. In addition to this, the proliferation of personal injury lawyers, all too keen to launch ever more compensation claims against anyone thought to be liable, has done much to increase employers' awareness of the need to safeguard their own position as much as the welfare of their employees.

Chapter Four

During my year as a messenger boy I learnt many things and began to develop the skills which would serve me well in the years to come. Harland & Wolff could reasonably be regarded as a training ground for the young and naive, a university of life containing a myriad of characters and experiences, all of which combined to shape and develop one's personality and ability to cope with whatever life chose to toss one's way in the future.

This eclectic mix of people obviously produced some who were good, some who were bad and some who were downright vicious, if not a little mad. Some of these 'characters' earned near legendary status for their exploits or madcap stunts; one such individual was Ronnie Cox, a huge bear of a man with a personality bordering on the psychotic, who truly deserved his fearsome reputation.

The son of an obscure diplomat, Ronnie had been indulged in almost every whim by his absentee parents, with the result that he regarded figures of authority as fair game to be abused as he saw fit. My first contact with 'Coxy', as he was universally known, was during the daily canteen run, when I went round the drawing office staff collecting their morning snack orders. Coxy had a voracious appetite, and each day purchased three bags of cheese and onion crisps, a Bar Six chocolate bar, two cooked ham baps and a carton of milk. This daily repast would be wolfed down in less than five minutes, while spraying crumbs and bits of food everywhere, much to the amazement and disgust of those on adjacent drawing boards. Because of his unusual feeding habits and unpredictable demeanour, nobody wanted to be seated next to him, with the result that any new arrival in the office invariably drew the short straw and found themselves next to the dreaded Coxy.

One such unfortunate individual was a very timid and extremely nervous elderly draughtsman named Will Waldron who, prior to his arrival in the office, had been regaled mercilessly by his erstwhile colleagues with blood-curdling tales of Coxy's mad behaviour. Unbeknown to Will, at the same time Coxy was being egged-on to play up to his reputation for lunacy, and so the scene was set for the predictable reaction. However, even those who had set the whole thing up could not have foreseen the dramatic outcome.

The morning routine was progressing easily enough, with each person busily engaged on their various tasks. Will had arrived in the office a week previously, and had been greatly relieved to find his partner sharing the drawing board to be a pleasant fellow, if a trifle odd, but nothing like the ogre he had been led to expect. Suddenly, and almost imperceptibly, he heard a strange, low growling noise which emanated from somewhere alongside him. Thinking he was imagining things he returned to his drawing when he heard it again, only louder this time. A slight movement caught his eye, and as he turned towards the sound he caught a glimpse of Coxy quickly closing his bench drawer, while at the same time wiping his mouth with the back of his hand. 'Alright Ronnie?' Will tentatively enquired, only to be answered by a grunted 'Aye, bit hungry that's all.'

Over the next half-hour the sequence of growling and drawer slamming was repeated, becoming louder and more prolonged each time. Subjected to such a protracted bout of tension, poor Will was by this time trembling with fright and barely able to retain his rather tenuous grip on reality. Suddenly, without warning, it happened: taking everyone by surprise with devastating effect, Ronnie ripped open his drawer and, plunging his hands inside, pulled out a large lump of meat, scarlet red and dripping with blood. With an almighty roar he thrust the meat towards his mouth and bit off a huge chunk of the flesh, which he proceeded to devour as the blood ran in crimson streams down his chin and onto his shirt. This shocking sight proved too much for Will's fragile nerves, and with a terrified scream he leapt almost vertically off his stool and ran as fast as he could out of the office. Unfortunately, in his blind panic, as he bolted out of the door and into the corridor he was unable to slow down enough to safely navigate the stairs and so plunged headlong down each flight until he eventually came to rest at the next floor. Sadly for him, his fall resulted in a broken arm, a fracture to his leg and several cuts and bruises necessitating several weeks off work. Coxy, of course, thought the whole incident hilarious, delighting in the fact that he had succeeded in absolutely terrifying such a timid and shy person. However, it left a rather bad taste in the mouths of the rest of the staff.

Over the ensuing months it became increasingly obvious that Coxy was developing an even more erratic streak to his behaviour, constantly challenging authority and generally acting in an irrational manner, until one day the inevitable confrontation with management occurred. Coxy had persistently and deliberately ignored the normal starting time for work, usually arriving into the office between twenty and thirty minutes late, whereupon he would strike the time clock with such force it invariably stopped. Despite receiving several warnings about his poor timekeeping, Coxy carried on regardless until he finally received a written warning that any further incidences would result in severe disciplinary action, i.e.

the sack. The next morning, as we waited with bated breath to see what effect this warning would have, Coxy, as usual, arrived some twenty minutes late, only this time carrying a loaded but broken shotgun over his arm. Striking the clock with his usual ferocity, he strode up the office to his drawing board and calmly laid the shotgun along the side of the bench. As the room held its breath, the Chief Draughtsman rose from his desk and began to make his way towards Coxy, until he noticed the shotgun that was. The colour rapidly drained from his face and, discretion being the better part of valour, he retreated back to his desk and sat down. Throughout the office you could have heard a pin drop as everyone busied themselves with their duties until, unable to contain his curiosity any longer, one of the office clerks asked Coxy if the gun was really loaded.

Without uttering a single word, Coxy picked up the shotgun, closed the breech and, pointing it downwards towards the concrete floor between the hapless clerk's feet, pulled the trigger. At once a tremendous blast echoed around the office as the startled and terrified clerk staggered backwards, his ears ringing from the shock of the noise. 'Jesus Christ, you could have killed me you mad bastard,' he said as he looked at the scene of devastation below him.

The outer edge of the pellet blast had sliced through the toecaps of his shoes, literally shredding the material, and by some great good fortune somehow missing doing the same to his toes. 'Look at my fucking shoes!' he yelled, his voice rising almost to screaming pitch as the full realisation of what had happened dawned on him. 'They're fucking ruined you great cunt. What the hell did you do that for?' Coxy simply looked at him with an unblinking stare for a few moments before slowly reaching out and grabbing him by the throat. We never knew precisely what it was that Coxy said to the clerk as he hissed into his ear, but whatever it was it was enough for him to suddenly calm down and scuttle back to his desk, where he remained, shaking, for the remainder of the morning.

Of course such a dramatic and shocking incident could not go unreported, and within a very short while a posse of Harland & Wolff security men accompanied by several harbour police officers arrived to investigate the incident. Much to our great surprise and relief, Coxy didn't put up any resistance when confronted by the small army who had arrived to remove him from the premises. There was momentary panic when he again picked up the shotgun, but thankfully he simply unloaded the remaining cartridge from the breech and handed the once-again broken weapon to the nearest policeman. Still without uttering a word, he slowly walked out of the office, albeit under close escort. A pair of boots was found for the still quivering clerk, who was allowed to go home at lunch time after providing a full statement of events. He then enjoyed a week's paid leave to recover from his trauma. Coxy spent a few months in hospital before returning to the company. However, a couple of months later he established a unique record in becoming the only person to have a redundancy notice issued solely for him, although even this simple act was not without its drama.

Coxy had realised a few weeks before that moves were being made to finally remove him from employment with the company. He was aware that his behaviour had gone from the mildly eccentric to almost lunatic, and as such could no longer be tolerated. Furthermore, his erstwhile colleagues had decided that they were no longer prepared to work with him. Faced with such complete opposition, the company had agreed with the draughtsmen's union to make Coxy redundant rather than sack him, which would be the usual procedure in these circumstances. The union had successfully pleaded that while Coxy's behaviour warranted instant dismissal, the immediate loss of income would cause him great hardship, and the stigma on his record would, in all probability, preclude him from gaining alternative employment. As a result of this arrangement, it fell upon Jack Gordon, the Chief Draughtsman, to issue Coxy with his redundancy notice, a task he was quite understandably dreading given Coxy's reputation for violence. Unknown to any of us, especially Jack, Coxy had taken to carrying a twelve-inch 'Bowie' knife, which he concealed in a scabbard behind his back. Coxy stood impassively in front of Jack's desk as he was informed of the reasons he was to be made redundant. However, as Jack passed the envelope containing the official notice, Coxy suddenly reached behind him and withdrew the knife from its scabbard. Waving it high in the air, he swiftly plunged it downwards towards the envelope lying on the desk with such force that the blade penetrated not only the envelope, but the desktop as well, right up to the hilt of the knife.

As can be imagined, Jack was completely terrified by this turn of events and had shot backwards in his chair as he watched the knife thud into his desk. He was still shaking as he heard Coxy say in a completely emotionless voice, 'I won't accept that,' before calmly turning on his heels and leaving the office. Of course, his refusal to accept the envelope was of little consequence as his fate had already been decided, and that evening he was escorted from the premises by several security men. As for the knife, it took the combined efforts of three of us pulling and straining to extract it from the top of Jack's desk. Coxy never returned to collect it and none of us had the nerve to return it to him personally. Jack never really recovered from the fright he had received, and developed a nervous tick and twitch whenever confronted with a stressful situation. He elected to stand down as Chief Draughtsman a few months after the incident and subsequently opted for early retirement a few years later.

Of course, not all the characters at Harland & Wolff were like Ronnie Cox, nor were such incidents commonplace. Most people were simply ordinary folk who found themselves in extraordinary circumstances. Among these many characters a few stood out from the rest. One such was 'Minger', who picked up his nickname after a particularly hard-fought football match. These matches took place in the steel stockyard each lunchtime, and usually involved teams of twenty or so players on each side. Unfortunately for Minger, this particular day he chanced to kick a steel plate rather than the ball, with the inevitable consequence that he broke a bone in his foot. Collapsing in agony, he rolled around the ground clutching his foot as we all gathered round to survey the damage. It quickly became obvious that he required immediate medical attention, and so, hoisting him up onto his good foot, he was half-carried, half-dragged to the company medical centre. As all ball games were strictly prohibited, his injury was reported as having been caused by a slip on the deck of a ship, without going into details as to why a message boy should be in such a location in the first place. The doctor duly appeared and instructed the nurse to remove Minger's sock and shoe to allow him to examine the injury, returning a few moments later only to find Minger apparently still wearing his sock.

'I told you to remove his sock nurse,' said the doctor, to which the nurse replied, 'His sock *is* off doctor: it's his feet that are that colour.' Sure enough, Minger's foot was as black as the ace of spades, encrusted in years of dirt and grime and stinking to high heaven. We didn't hang about to see what happened next, but from then on this poor soul would be forever known as 'Minger', and we always made sure he kept his boots on at all times. A popular rumour at the time alleged that his feet were so bad they had to be sand-blasted to remove the dirt before the doctor would touch him, and his socks had to be beaten to death with a stick. Whatever the truth of the matter, he did eventually return with his foot in a plaster cast, but we never did find out what became of his socks.

'Budgie' arrived on his first day bedecked in a luminous bright-yellow sweater, looking for all the world like a rather over-stuffed canary, and of course he was immediately christened Budgie. Not one of nature's most industrious creatures, Budgie indulged in regular days off, employing ever more elaborate excuses to explain his regular absences.

This came to a head one day when Budgie found himself attempting to explain yet another absence to an increasingly sceptical Chief Draughtsman. Engrossed as he was in recounting his tale of woe, he was disconcerted to see his supervisor break into a wide grin and appear to find some amusement in his sorry saga. By now desperately struggling to stifle a laugh, the supervisor dismissed Budgie with a cursory wave of his hand, indicating that he should return to his drawing board. As he turned to leave the glazed inner office and rejoin his peers, Budgie was horrified to see several of us holding up the type of numbered cards often seen at ice skating events to indicate the judges' scores. Budgie never forgave us for 'scoring' his performance, but at least he earned a commendable 8.5 for presentation and 9.8 for content.

The layout and construction of the office itself led to various high jinks as, being Victorian in design, it had very high ceilings supported by massive square pillars. A popular challenge issued to all new recruits was to climb one of these pillars in the gent's washroom and place their footprint on the ceiling. Budgie simply couldn't resist this challenge and before an appreciative audience proceeded to climb the pillar. He had just reached the top when Sam Kirkpatrick, the new Chief Draughtsman, entered the washroom to use the urinal. At his arrival most of us scattered, but I was one of the few to remain as I was washing my hands at the time. Sam came over to the sink beside me and proceeded to wash his hands. As he did so a slight whimper could be heard from high above as Budgie struggled to retain his grip on the pillar. Unfortunately for him, Sam decided to enjoy some fresh air, and after drying his hands opened the window and leant on the window sill. Just at that precise moment, Budgie lost both his battle with gravity and his grip on the pillar to drop like a stone, landing directly behind Sam with a tremendous smack on the tiled floor.

Startled out of his wits, Sam banged the back of his head on the window above him. 'Where the hell did you come from?' he asked. 'Ah sorry boss, I tripped on the way over here,' replied Budgie, desperately trying to keep his voice steady while struggling to overcome the burning agony from the soles of his feet. 'I'll just go back in the office now,' he said, turning towards the door, every step sending a searing pain from his feet through his body as he made his painful exit. 'Boy's bloody mad,' muttered Sam as he returned to the window once again, adding, 'No wonder he tripped, by the way he walks that lad must have terrible trouble with his feet.'

My time in the drawing office was rapidly drawing to a close, and all too soon I would be transferred to the Apprentice Training Centre to begin my apprenticeship. However, as fate would decree, I would, in later years, return to this environment to continue my career. Although I could not imagine at that exact moment the path that fate would eventually lead me, it was with a heavy heart that I took my leave of the good friends I had made among the draughtsmen and office staff. I would carry with me the memories of the everyday fun and games, and the plots and schemes forever being hatched between the various drawing offices, each department striving to outdo the other with ever more elaborate schemes or cons, a prime example being the 'great shirt swindle'.

As with all con tricks, the element of greed plays a vital role in the successful outcome of the sting, and on this occasion the chosen target was a particularly avaricious, and therefore rather disliked, individual. Well known for his tight-fisted behaviour, propensity to borrow everything from money to personal items, and lax attitude towards returning them without several reminders, he made the ideal target. The fact that he was also the most nosey and inquisitive individual I have ever met only added to the pleasure when the trap set for him was eventually closed. To save his embarrassment should he ever read this, I shall refer to him simply as Davy.

It all began innocently enough when one of the draughtsmen brought some boxed shirts into the office and was showing them to a colleague during the lunch break. Snooping about the office as always, Davy spotted the shirt boxes and, always interested in a potential bargain, invited himself into the conversation. Much to his delight he discovered that the boxes contained shirts manufactured by top brand names Van Heusen and Peter England; more to the point they were available at a third of the price they normally retailed at in the shops. To allay his suspicions, it was explained to Davy that while the shirts were perfect, as the couple he examined indeed were, they had actually 'fallen off the back of a lorry', and were therefore available as a once-only offer, strictly cash sale and no returns. Davy's mind immediately went into overdrive at the prospect of making a killing; his sister owned a small outfitters and as such presented him with the perfect opportunity to cash in on his apparent good fortune. The fact that his sister would be selling what, in effect, was stolen property, never entered his mind, so intent was he on getting his greedy hands on as many shirts as he could. Obviously, given the nature of supply, the number of shirts available was not unlimited. However, after much urging and cajoling, Davy eventually persuaded the vendor to let him have six dozen shirts in whatever sizes and colours were available. Eager to seal the arrangement, he slipped away from work that very afternoon to the bank and withdrew the £350 necessary to finance the transaction.

Always loath to part with money, Davy was on tenterhooks until the next morning when, much to his obvious relief, he was shown the seventy-two boxes of shirts safely under a blanket in the back of the vendor's car. Opening a few boxes at random to satisfy himself that they did actually contain shirts, he could barely contain his excitement as he eagerly transferred the shirts to his car and covered them up. By mid-morning his greed had overtaken him, and he again slipped away from the office to deliver the shirts to his sister's shop; all he had to do now was sit back and count his profit. That was until the telephone call came from his sister.

Shortly after Davy had delivered the shirts, his sister had sold one to a customer who was now standing before her extremely angry and demanding his money back. He was not amused to have discovered, when he unpacked the shirt, that it comprised nothing more than a collar and shirt front. Far from being a complete shirt, all he had actually obtained was a trade item supplied to undertakers for the purpose of dressing a corpse prior to burial or cremation.

The colour drained from Davy's face and his hands began to tremble as his sister went on to explain that she had examined all the boxes and found every one to be the same – not one contained an actual complete shirt. As Davy struggled to comprehend the devastating news, all around him the office erupted in laughter as we realised that he had just discovered what we already knew. He did get his money back some weeks later, but only after an anxious wait, having been told that it had been paid over to a paramilitary organisation who had been the alleged supplier of the shirts in the first place. Of course, such entrepreneurial business acumen was not confined solely to the drawing offices; one manager in particular ran such a successful business empire from his shipyard office that he became universally known as the 'White Pakistani'. So widespread and diverse were his operations that he couldn't afford to spend much time actually on the premises of Harland & Wolff. Should any activity occur requiring his attendance he would be telephoned at home by his clerk, whereupon he would go to the shipyard and deal with the situation before returning to his more profitable activities.

For several years the Staging Department had run a very lucrative and successful sideline in all manner of consumer goods. Their equipment store was a veritable Aladdin's cave of merchandise, from video recorders and television sets to designer label clothing. Such was the slickness of this operation, a small area equipped with several full-length mirrors had been set aside at the rear of the store to enable prospective customers to try on their choice of outfit before purchase. Orders could be placed for specific items, in particular toys and games for children, while anything not in stock could usually be obtained within a few days. In some cases items would be manufactured to individual specification within the shipyard itself, a useful facility when one of the most popular items was a child's wooden horse. I recall being in the store browsing the latest merchandise when a message boy arrived to place an order for several of these toys. Standing at the 'counter' which had been roughly assembled from a number of staging planks, he announced in the strongest Belfast brogue I had ever heard, 'I want ten aff dem wooden horses, six wee wheels and four wee runners, dem ones wit da wheels till be painted white, and dem ones wid only da runners just to be left varnished, dat OK then?' The Stager, leaning languidly across the counter, replied, 'Aye, I'll just put it in the book,' and, brushing aside a pile of ship's construction drawings, uncovered a thick ledger. Without even allowing him a second glance, the order was solemnly recorded into the ledger and a delivery date given for sometime the following week. As the messenger turned to leave, he was reminded by the surly-looking individual who had accepted his order, 'Cash on delivery mind and no cancellations. Just be sure you bring the right money when you come back because if not we'll be lookin for you, understand?' 'Aye right enough, see ye next week,' he replied as he left the store. In reality this order, together with those for similar items that could be manufactured in-house, would be passed on to their 'sub-contractor', which in this case was the shipyard's own Joiners Shop, where they would be produced in near assembly line conditions.

Lines of supply were also established with other departments, for example the Blacksmiths Shop, where a complete range of items from simple pokers to fabulous wrought-iron gates and fence panels were produced, or the Sheetmetal Shop, where toy cars, trains and boats were manufactured to the highest standards. The items produced by this 'cottage industry' were every bit as good, if not frequently far better, than those available commercially, which is a tribute to the first-rate skills these men possessed in their various trades. Had Harland & Wolff ever considered producing these items as officially sanctioned products, they may have had more commercial success with this type of venture than they enjoyed from their core business.

While this method of shopping had its obvious advantages, the major drawback was that nothing could be returned or taken for repair if it failed to operate. In particular, customers were warned never to send off the guarantee registration card for their video. If it went wrong the advice was to 'throw it over a hedge or get a mate to look at it for ye'. As one may have expected in such circumstances, the Electrical Manufacturing Department were happy to provide a repair service for such items, strictly cash terms (of course!) and don't ask for a receipt. The senior management of the company were well aware of this lucrative sideline and tried on several occasions to close down the operations. These attempts met with absolutely no success whatsoever and were eventually abandoned as a pointless exercise, probably because those charged with the task of eradicating these activities were in all likelihood its best customers, and were supplementing their already large salaries by selling on many of the items to their friends and neighbours.

Chapter Five

My arrival at the Apprentice Training Centre meant a complete change of atmosphere from that which I had experienced as a message boy. Gone was the leisurely pace of life and the opportunity for fun and laughter with your colleagues, replaced instead by the austere discipline of structured activities reinforced by constant supervision and assessment. After experiencing almost a full year among the draughtsmen and engineers in the company's main offices, the reality of the world I now found myself in came as a major culture shock, particularly given my somewhat sensitive disposition and the nature of my upbringing. The start of my apprenticeship had propelled me into the sharp end of life in Harland & Wolff, and I quickly discovered that the working conditions endured by the 'blue collar' employees were far removed from those I had experienced during my time as a member of the office staff. Suddenly I was faced with countless rules and regulations, very few of which made any apparent sense and the majority of which seemed unnecessarily harsh in both practice and implementation, almost to the point of inhumanity. Given the myriad of regulations which today ensure a minimum permitted standard of working conditions, it is difficult to believe such strict conditions were either allowed to exist or could have been tolerated in a civilised society.

Many of these rules were petty in the extreme and were designed simply as a means to exercise an unreasonable amount of control over the employees. It is very likely that this culture of brutality had its roots in the earliest years of Harland & Wolff. Certainly Edward Harland was famous for once sacking the entire workforce and could not abide any form of organised labour. He preferred to exert his will by the use of fear and intimidation, to the point that he would frequently have someone dismissed simply to demonstrate his absolute power over his workforce. Wolff, on the other hand, took a much more pragmatic approach to company discipline, laying down strict rules governing dress and conduct to be observed by the office staff. Anyone found falling foul of his orders would find themselves faced with a system of suspensions ranging from one week to three months. He was acutely aware that he could not afford to dismiss any draughtsmen if he was to maintain the design and drawing schedules being demanded by Edward Harland. He preferred the 'short sharp shock' method, whereby a transgressor could be punished without being permanently lost to the workforce. In these early years qualified draughtsmen were particularly difficult to replace, especially draughtsmen familiar with marine-type activities. Shipyards on the mainland could source replacement draughtsmen from other yards, but Harland & Wolff was at that time the only shipyard in Northern Ireland, and as such had no easily available pool of skilled labour to draw upon.

Successive company Chairmen were schooled to follow Edward Harland's harsh example, and indeed his successor, Lord Pirrie, simply regarded everyone else as having an inferior intellect to his own and would consequently completely ignore any piece of advice or dissenting opinion offered to him. Pirrie proceeded to run the company almost as a personal fiefdom, refusing to share any of his decisions or his thinking behind them with the other directors. Indeed, when Harland & Wolff faced a financial crisis, such was Pirrie's secrecy that even the Chief Accountant was denied access to the company accounts and the chance to determine the solvency of the company. Pirrie would meet with prospective ship owners in complete secrecy and agree a price for the vessel. He would then oversee every aspect of the financial arrangements, confining himself to providing the Chief Accountant with a note of the profit or loss. It appears incredible that a major company should be run in this fashion, but, such was Pirrie's personal presence on the Board, that any challenge to his methods or authority was unthinkable. Pirrie's attitude to the workforce was one of almost complete indifference bordering on contempt; during his frequent inspections of the vessels under construction he would often order that workers be dismissed for such petty infringements as whistling or yawning. He contended that anyone whistling could not be concentrating 100 per cent on his duties, while having the temerity to yawn indicated an inherent laziness and slovenly attitude.

A typical example of these insensitive regulations was the rule governing the use of the lavatory by manual workers. During my time in the offices the lavatories had been available for use as and when required. However, I now found myself faced with the stipulation that no more than seven minutes per day were allowed to answer the call of nature. To enforce this regulation, each lavatory had a clerk stationed at the entrance to each toilet block whose duty was to record the board number and time of arrival of each user. They, of course, were universally known as 'shit house clerks', and among their duties they had to ensure strict adherence to the time limit by calling out a person's board number with the reminder that, 'Yer seven minutes is up an' you are now shittin' in yer own time'. Anyone who found themselves in the unfortunate position of being unable to complete their ablutions within the allotted time found their board number reported to the timekeepers and their wages deducted accordingly, usually by a minimum of thirty minutes. Because of this, many employees simply performed their bodily functions where they were working rather than face the inevitable financial penalty a visit to the lavatory could incur. As can be imagined, this in turn led to rather unsavoury working conditions and added to the already dirty and unsanitary atmosphere.

The toilets themselves were somewhat spartan in appearance and function; they were little more than ramshackle buildings providing the basic minimum of sanitation. Each lavatory block consisted of a number of stalls, each positioned over a continuous metal trough and closed off by a wooden door of no more than three feet in height. These doors, being so short, ensured that each patron could be seen at all times and therefore would not be tempted to use the lavatory for any purpose other than that for which it was intended. However, as these facilities also usually lacked any protection from the elements, it was difficult to believe they would be a place anyone would wish to linger in the first place.

Freezing cold in winter, fetid and stinking in high summer, only the truly desperate or perhaps foolhardy braved these dreadful conditions. On the other hand, many of the more experienced employees chose to avoid them for another more straightforward reason. By their basic method of construction, the lavatories presented an open section at the back of the toilet block, about a foot wide and directly above the trough. Anyone passing the rear of the facility could clearly see the exposed backside of anyone using the lavatory and this presented them with a golden opportunity to engage in some mischief. In normal circumstances it would be the apprentices who were proved to be the perpetrators of such monkey business, perhaps in an early attempt to establish some sort of tough reputation.

The most common prank carried out on the unwary was to sneak up to the rear of the latrine and violently strike any bare backside with a piece of timber, leaving a large red welt across the buttocks of the unfortunate victim. However, it was not unknown for an even more disgusting trick to be played. This involved the perpetrator inserting the piece of wood between the lavatory trough and his victim's backside, thus intercepting the faecal matter on the end of the wood, this was then thrust upward smearing the unsuspecting victim with his own faeces. Such behaviour was commonplace among the apprentices, who would seek out new methods in which to outdo each other. Anyone who found themselves unable or unwilling to cope with such behaviour found themselves isolated, and invariably the target of ever more vicious stunts.

Many of those being accepted for apprenticeships had not previously been employed by Harland & Wolff as message boys, rather they had arrived straight from school, or in some cases direct from the unemployment register. While the company would have much preferred all of its apprentice intake to have passed 'through the ranks' as message boys, and therefore have had the chance to assess the individual character of each candidate over a period of time, in reality this was impossible to achieve. The number of apprentice vacancies each year far outnumbered the available places for message boys, with the result that the majority of new apprentices had no experience or knowledge of the company. This imbalance created a certain amount of friction between the two groups, to the degree that an atmosphere of simmering resentment soon developed into open hostility which frequently resulted in fist fights and violence.

Such behaviour simply served to reinforce the sense of clannishness we felt and exacerbated our less positive characteristics. It is probably an over-simplification to say we were brutalised by such an atmosphere, but we did learn very quickly how to protect ourselves and self-preservation became paramount. Those who would not, or simply could not, adapt to this bleak environment of belligerence and aggression, quickly fell by the wayside as the constant atmosphere of brutality took its toll on the meek and mild among us. Personally, I found the whole experience absolute hell and detested every day I had to endure it. However, I had little choice but to put aside my private feelings and press on as best I could.

My father had always wanted me to obtain an apprenticeship; to him an unskilled man had wasted his opportunities in life and was therefore beneath contempt. For me then, resigning was definitely not an option, not if I wanted a quiet life at home. However, I did talk to him about what I was experiencing, but with little effect. He simply reminded me of his own hardships as an apprentice and that what I was experiencing now would strengthen my character and make a man of me. Eventually, however, I would find the courage to follow my convictions and did abandon my apprenticeship to make my own future.

The catalyst for my decision came after a particularly difficult week at work, in which several minor injuries had occurred as the result of some especially vicious shenanigans between the various groups of apprentices. Working at my small bench on a rather complex test piece, I received a tap on my shoulder. Thinking it was the instructor I looked up, only to have a paint brush soaked in red lead preservative thrust forcibly into my face. A searing pain immediately shot through both my eyes as the chemical splashed into them, burning the delicate surface like the sting of a thousand bees. Blinded and terrified I sank to my knees, desperately rubbing at the agonising smarting in my eyes. 'Don't rub them son,' came the voice of my instructor from somewhere behind me, 'You'll only make it worse. Try and stand up.'

1 *Right:* First year apprentice training in the Queens Shipyard of Harland & Wolff, located outside the rear entrance of the main company offices. Left to right: Jackie Snodden, Tom (Tommy) McCluskie and Bertie Gaibraith.

2 *Below:* Nothing remains of the magnificent Harland & Wolff Engine Works except weeds and memories of what used to be.

3 Silent and abandoned: Harland & Wolff's main entrance in Summer 2004. All these buildings have subsequently been demolished to make way for redevelopment of the site.

Above and opposite above: 4, 5 This is all that remains of the Harland & Wolff main Drawing Offices and Queens Shipyard, birthplace of the *Titanic* and many other famous vessels.

6 View of the Queens Road which runs through the heart of Harland & Wolff. This road once echoed to the tramp of 38,000 men, but today it is deserted.

Above and left: 7, 8 The Thompson dry-dock, birthplace of the RMS *Titanic.* Today it lies derelict and forlorn.

Opposite above: 9 Band of the 1st Battalion Royal Irish Regiment entertaining the American visitors at the gala dinner in Harland & Wolff.

10 Gala dinner for the *Titanic* Historical Society held in Harland & Wolff's main function room on 12 April 1996. The author's wife Sylvia is facing the camera on the left of the photograph.

Above: 11 Flags welcoming the first batch of American visitors to Harland & Wolff.

Left: 12 The same scene today, neglected, sad and overgrown with weeds.

Right: 13 The author hard at work! Harland & Wolff Technical Services, September 1996.

Below and overleaf: 14, 15 The author receiving his MBE for services to the RMS *Titanic* and maritime history, 24 November 2004.

Above: 16 Laying the keel of another new vessel; Musgrave Shipyard, 1965.

Right: 17 Installing the funnel on MV *Port St Lawrence*. In the past several men were crushed during such operations. The gang of men were required to stand beneath the funnel as it was lowered to ensure that it landed in the correct place. On at least three occasions that I know of men lost their toes as the funnel trapped their feet and cut through their boots as it descended.

Placing his hands underneath my armpits, he lifted me to my feet and tried to reassure me that everything would be fine. 'It's not too bad son, just a bit has gone into your eyes, but the medical centre will soon sort that out for you,' and with that he placed his arm around my shoulders and led me towards the help I desperately needed. As I stumbled along, unable to open my eyes, my heart was pounding from the shock of what had just happened. I had never before felt as frightened and alone as I did then, terrified that my eyes had suffered some permanent damage, or indeed that I might even be blind. I struggled to contain the tears that began to stream down my face. Eventually we reached the door of the medical centre and I was ushered in to receive the urgent treatment I required for my injury. 'What the hell happened to him?' asked the male nurse on duty. 'Fucking about as usual I suppose?' He then answered his own question by adding: 'Ah no, bit of an accident with a tin of paint.' With disbelief I realised that once again the unwritten code of Harland & Wolff was being exercised.

The code was simple: nobody ever, EVER, reported any misbehaviour to anyone in authority. Like the Mafia code of silence, breaking this unwritten rule would result in dire consequences for the complainant. In shipyard terms this would range from simple things like your lunch box going missing or laxative being slipped into your tea, to extreme measures like damage to your vehicle or sabotage of the job you were working on. Neither was it uncommon for those who, for whatever reason, had broken this unwritten rule, to find themselves high on the list of the next batch of redundancies to take place.

As the nurse cleaned my burning eyes I silently resolved that enough was enough – nothing was worth the misery I was experiencing every day. I simply could no longer contemplate learning a trade I had come to hate among people I detested. 'I don't think there is any permanent damage son,' said the nurse kindly, as he flushed saline solution across my eyes. 'I'll just need some details for the accident book.' Despite my pain and anger I was astute enough to realise that this was not the time to break the code.

'The paint tin just spilt when I opened it,' I lied, 'and it got into my eyes.' This excuse was so improbable it was obviously a deliberate lie, nevertheless that was what was recorded in the accident book, and to all intents and purposes was the end of the matter. Two weeks later, without a second backward glance, I walked out of the training centre for the last time, having secured a job in the local firm of R.E. Hamilton & Co. They were one of the main Ford dealerships in Belfast and would show me that not everywhere was as archaic as Harland & Wolff.

My father was of course furious that I had, in his words, 'thrown away a good trade for no good reason', and unfortunately this created a gulf between us that would take several years to repair. My mother, on the other hand, took a more pragmatic view of things and was totally unconcerned at the abrupt change of career, taking the simplistic view that as long as I was happy and in full-time employment she could not see the problem.

My engineering background, such as it was, stood me in good stead for my new employment, and I commenced work in the Parts Department at R.E. Hamilton's central Belfast garage. I quickly settled down into a comfortable routine, and before long felt completely at home. The atmosphere was relaxed and friendly, a complete world away from the harsh reality I had so recently escaped. Coming as I did from Harland & Wolff I found myself the butt of the usual jokes such as 'how many men work in the shipyard?' answer 'about half of them'. However, these jibes were in good humour and no malice was ever intended. My time spent working at R.E. Hamilton's would result in another, even more dramatic impact on my life, an impact I could not possibly have anticipated or even imagined at the time.

The day was much like any other. The Parts Department was busy, but not unusually so, when one of my colleagues answered a routine phone call. The caller was enquiring if we had in stock an exhaust silencer for a Ford Anglia, and if so how much would it cost? Confirming that we did indeed have one available, my colleague Ronnie said that it would be left aside for collection, and to be sure that the right part was supplied the person collecting it was to ask for him when they arrived. About an hour later a very attractive and petite brunette arrived to collect the part. However, on seeing that it was over six feet in length and covered in a protective film of grease she asked if it was possible for it to be delivered.

I had seen the young lady earlier that morning in the local café we used for our morning break. She had been standing in front of me in the queue and I couldn't help but notice that she possessed the most fabulous pair of legs I had ever seen. However, being relatively shy I simply hadn't the courage to speak to her despite the frenetic encouragement of my companions.

Returning to work after our break, my companions took great delight in compounding my embarrassment by quickly spreading the word to the rest of my colleagues about my failure to chat up such a good-looking girl, a girl who I had obviously taken quite a fancy to. Much to their delight and my obvious chagrin I had to endure their merciless, but nevertheless good-natured, ribbing about 'faint hearts never winning fair ladies' and so on *ad nauseam*. Suddenly, there she was again standing right in front of me, but I still faced the same problem of how to break the ice, a problem made worse by the fact that those who had been with me that morning and had recognised her made sure everyone else knew she had been the object of my desire. As fate would have it, the problem resolved itself as Ronnie, my colleague who had taken the order for the silencer, offered my services in delivering it to her place of work. Of course his decision was influenced by the fact that my discomfort at once again coming face to face with the young lady was clearly evident for all to see.

Taking me to one side he hissed into my ear, 'You have a second chance to chat her up and get a date for the night, so mind you don't cock it up this time.' Turning to the young lady he said, 'Don't worry love, young Rufus (my nickname) will take it round for you, just be sure and send him back the way you found him.' With that he thrust the silencer into my hand and pushed me round the counter towards the front door. However he could not resist adding to my discomfiture by saying, 'Just you behave yourself now, and make sure you keep them hands to yourself.'

Relieved and delighted to at last be away from all the banter, we walked along towards the end of the street. Realising I didn't have a clue where I was going presented me with the opportunity to speak directly to her for the first time. Stumbling over the words, I found out where we were headed and, taking a very deep breath and my courage in both hands, blurted out, 'My name's Tom by the way,' to which she replied, 'That's a lovely name, mine's Sylvia.' Walking along together we began to chat. However, desperate as I was to ask her out I simply could not find the courage to do so, and all too soon we arrived at her workplace where I meekly handed over the silencer to her boss, and with a feeble wave said goodbye. As I trudged miserably back to R.E. Hamilton's, I cursed myself for being so lily-livered and throwing away what had been a golden opportunity to ask her out, not to mention dreading the inevitable teasing I would receive from my friends. All too soon I found myself back outside the front door of the Parts Department, and, taking a deep breath, opened it and went in, resigned to facing the worst – only for fate to throw me yet another chance.

Ronnie greeted me with, 'Christ lad you must have made some impression. They've asked you to go back and tell her boss how to fit that bloody silencer. I think it's only an excuse for the rest of yon wee lassy's mates to get a good look at you.' Unable to believe what I was hearing, my heart leapt at the opportunity to see Sylvia again, and this time nothing was going to stop me asking her out. 'Get yerself away back there. It's OK, I've cleared it with Dessie (the manager) but don't be all day about it.' I fairly galloped back to where Sylvia worked and this time made sure I grasped the opportunity to ask her out. Much to my delight, she accepted.

From that moment onwards we were constantly together and have never looked back. Seven years later we were married in the beautiful country church she had attended since she was a little girl. Recalling those early years, I often wonder at just how extraordinary fate can be. Had I not decided to leave Harland & Wolff when I did I would never have had the opportunity to meet my future wife, and my life would have been so very much different. It never ceases to amaze me how such relatively minor changes in our everyday lives can ultimately have such profound effects and alter our future course in such dramatic ways. A slight variance in one's normal routine can sometimes result in devastating consequences or amazing good fortune. Simply leave home five minutes later than your usual time and you may find yourself involved in a tragic accident, or maybe by the simple act of missing your bus you could be destined to meet for the first time the love of your life. Such apparently random occurrences can be nothing more than a simple quirk of fate, or the Gods amusing themselves by changing the course of your life in the blink of an eye. Whatever the truth of the matter, from such a seemingly insignificant event the course of your life is changed forever and nothing is ever the same again.

The remainder of my career in R.E. Hamilton's was relatively uneventful, with the usual mix of highs and lows that are commonly experienced by everyone who finds themselves working in a large organisation. During my time there I learnt several valuable lessons in the art of dealing with people, perhaps the most important being the ability to respond to difficult situations in a pragmatic and positive manner. The ability to stand back from a problem and take the time to think the situation through in a logical and rational manner would serve me well in the years to come. While I had enjoyed five very happy years working in R.E. Hamilton's, conditions there were slowly beginning to change. Trading had become difficult and talk of the company losing its Ford franchise became more pervasive with each passing day. Rumours also abounded that the company was about be sold to another dealership, which did nothing to foster staff morale or confidence in the future. Sadly, as I pondered the changing circumstances all around me, I realised that my future prospects had to be paramount in my thinking. I was now in a steady and committed relationship, which necessitated getting a job which would offer career prospects and a degree of security. With such thoughts uppermost in my mind, providence again intervened to change the course and direction of my life almost full circle – to the extent that I would find myself returning to Harland & Wolff, only this time I determined things would be very different – very different indeed.

Chapter Six

Going back to Harland & Wolff after such a long absence was a rather strange experience. In many ways if felt as if I had only been away for a few weeks on holiday, such was the familiarity of the surroundings. As I once again walked about the Queens Shipyard, my former mail route as a message boy, I was somehow not surprised to find that it was still the same cold and forbidding place it had always been. I would have imagined that after an absence of just over five years I would have seen some changes, not least to the primitive working conditions and facilities. Yet if I was to be perfectly honest with myself, I had to acknowledge that I simply didn't know what I thought I expected to find. Above me the towering hulks of the vessels under construction soared high into an overcast, grey sky surrounded by the framework of the crane gantries, stark against the backdrop of the green hills that surround Belfast on the far side of the river Lagan. Even the men who bustled back and forth from the slipways appeared to have remained the same, each face retaining that unmistakable, and yet so familiar, gaunt and haunted expression I had seen so often before. A popular myth about Belfast was that you could always tell if a man worked in the shipyard simply by looking at his face; nobody else looked as tired and drawn as those who earned their living building the big ships. As I stood there in those instantly recognisable surroundings, slowly letting the atmosphere begin to overwhelm me, I suddenly began to experience a strange and unnerving emotion. Almost imperceptibly, a feeling of reassurance pervaded every fibre of my being, almost as if I was returning to the comfort and security of my home after a long and arduous journey. The overwhelming sensation was one of warmth and contentment as the realisation gradually dawned upon me that this was the place where I truly belonged, where my heart had really been for all these years, I had at last come home.

I had returned to employment with Harland & Wolff as a technical administrator, and took up my post in the hull drawing office which, extraordinarily enough, was located in the old naval drawing office I had served in as a message boy. In an even more bizarre coincidence, the desk I was allocated was the one I had used previously as a mail sorting table. Despite this overwhelming feeling of *déjà vu*, I realised that the circumstances of my new position were very much different from those of the carefree existence I had previously enjoyed. I now had responsibility for ensuring the smooth running of the drawing office, by overseeing everything from the supply of pencils to ensuring the detailed construction drawings were approved by the ships' owners and the necessary regulatory bodies. These were usually Lloyds Register of Shipping and the Board of Trade Marine Surveyors Department.

Completion of this task proved on several occasion to be much more easily said than done; frequent conflicts arose between the various vested interests, with each party determined to impress upon everyone else their particular opinion. I often found myself in the role of referee between these various factions, and rapidly learnt to develop the diplomatic skills that would be so useful in the latter years of my career. As the shipbuilder, our first priority had to be to our customer, after all, they were the one who paid for our services. On the other hand, we simply could not afford to upset the regulatory bodies too much, as they had the ability to slow down ship production almost to a standstill by doggedly adhering to every requirement of their various regulations. By the judicious application of diplomacy and, when necessary, sheer bloody-mindedness, I usually managed to reach a compromise that everybody could accept. Of course this sometimes created problems for the construction trades when it came to actually building the vessel, but we got around this simply by reverting to our original arrangement without bothering to inform the owner or either of the other regulatory bodies. Occasionally this subterfuge would be discovered, resulting in profuse apologies for our error and the promise to put matters right, which we did if it was rather too obvious, otherwise we simply carried on regardless.

The interpersonal skills I had developed while in R.E. Hamilton's served me well on these occasions, and I quickly became adept at negotiating a safe course out of tricky situations. During this time I acquired the reputation of being a 'safe pair of hands', and thus began to come to the attention of the senior management in the department. I had rapidly progressed through the ranks of my contemporaries and found myself appointed as senior administrator a few years after rejoining the company. This speedy elevation did not go unnoticed by my peers, and not for the first time I began to encounter resentment and bitterness at my advancement from some of my erstwhile colleagues. The bitter experience I had endured when an apprentice had remained with me, much like a festering sore that cannot be soothed, and I had always regretted the fact that I did not display more grit and determination towards my antagonists at the time. When I returned to Harland & Wolff, my first resolve was that whatever provocation I encountered, I would meet it with determination and fortitude. Never again would I take the easy option and walk away from a challenge. If someone wanted a fight, well they could have one, but this time I would make sure I was the victor. The first test of my new resolve came a few months later, with news of the impending retirement of the Chief Administrator, a position of great power and influence in the Technical Departments. Several of my colleagues had their eye on this top job, but unbeknown to them the successor had already been selected, and at the time was not even working in the Technical Department.

Some months previously I had been seconded to the company Finance Department in order to gain a general working knowledge of the financial aspects of the business. To my former colleagues it appeared that I had simply obtained a transfer to the Finance Department for a higher salary and to further my ambitions. However, nothing could have been further from the truth. In actual fact my apparent transfer was nothing more than a secondment, and I therefore remained a Technical Department employee; more to the point I was soon to return as the new Chief Administrator.

Some time earlier I had been called to a meeting with the Chief Technical Manager, who had outlined his strategy to ensure smooth continuity within his department when the Chief Administrator retired. He went on to explain that he wanted me to consider accepting the position. However, if I did so it would mean a period away from the Technical Department for me to acquire the additional skills necessary to perform this role. In conclusion, he said I was to go away and consider the offer and, if I was wiling to undertake the task ahead, come back and let him know. I didn't need to go away and think about his offer. This position represented the top rung of the ladder in my field, and without a second's hesitation I accepted. What was there to think about? This was the job everybody wanted and it was now mine.

For weeks speculation had been rife among the various administrators about just who would succeed the Chief Administrator, to the extent that bets had been placed among the staff as to which of the candidates were most likely to succeed. The reaction to the announcement of my appointment as Chief Administrator was one of shock and stunned silence, bordering on disbelief. Here was someone they had discounted as a candidate suddenly reappearing as their immediate supervisor, and several years their junior to boot. Most of the staff took the news with stoicism and accepted the inevitable, albeit with little grace, nevertheless for one individual the news of my appointment was nothing short of devastating. He had been the firm favourite for the position, both in his own mind and that of his colleagues, and as such he reacted with fury when the announcement of my appointment was made. In typical Harland & Wolff style his anger was further fuelled by the barbed jibes he was forced to endure from almost every quarter as his discomfiture and humiliation became ever more evident.

For a few days I decided to tolerate the situation by allowing matters to cool down naturally. Unfortunately the anger and resentment felt by my rival only increased and this could result only in the kind of clash I had been so hoping to avoid.

By the fourth day in my new position, matters had deteriorated to such an extent that I was beginning to receive complaints from the various Chief Draughtsmen that their administrative staff were becoming truculent and rather argumentative with each other. I had sensed this air of discontent, but not wishing to be seen to overreact so early in my post I had decided to wait and see if things would improve over time. Sadly, my hopes of an improvement in the general atmosphere were ill-founded, and the situation had deteriorated to such an extent that I was left with no other choice than to take the bull by the horns and resolve the issue once and for all.

I was only too well aware that the source of the discontent was my main rival for this position, and in an effort to bring this difficult state of affairs to a rapid conclusion I invited him to my office to discuss the issue and hopefully resolve it. Unfortunately, my offer of an olive branch was rejected out of hand and I was brusquely informed that he did not accept my authority nor would he obey any instructions I would give to him. I must admit to being shocked by such hostility and open defiance and I cautioned him to very carefully consider his position. I made it abundantly clear to him that if he chose to continue with this course of action he would be wise to consider the consequences.

Much to my disappointment he again refused to recognise my authority or accept my instructions. Faced with such an intractable attitude I had no other option than to bring him before the Chief Technical Manager, who immediately brought the matter to a rapid and rather brutal conclusion. At what proved to be an extremely brief meeting, my rival was given the opportunity to outline his objections to my appointment. In particular he resented the fact that he had not even been granted the courtesy of an interview for the position, nor been provided with an explanation as to why he had been overlooked for what he considered was his job by virtue of his length of service within the department. A pregnant pause filled the room until, fixing my adversary with a cold and unwavering stare, the Chief Technical Manager finally spoke. With an inflection in his voice that would cut steel, he curtly advised the hapless administrator before him that in actual fact he had briefly been considered as a candidate for the post, only to be rejected simply because he was judged incapable of reaching the required standards. Furthermore, as Chief Technical Manager he saw absolutely no need to discuss or explain any of his decisions with a minor member of his staff, and had no intention of doing so, either now or at any time in the future.

After making sure the gravity of his remarks had been fully understood, he brought the short meeting to a close by informing my rival that if he continued to have difficulty in accepting the situation, he would expect him to place his resignation on my desk by the end of that day. Shocked by the abrupt manner in which his objections had been brushed aside, and visibly shaking from the experience, he almost bolted from the room, a sadder but also now wiser individual. Unfortunately, I also realised that this slap-down would be unlikely to see an end to hostilities between us. I had made an enemy in this individual, but one that I was confident I could neutralise as and when the occasion demanded it. However, the experience had taught me a valuable lesson about the exercise of authority, and as I returned to my office I recalled the words the Chief Technical Manager had said to me on my appointment: 'You have crossed the line between them and us now, and because of that you can no longer be "one of the boys" anymore. You are on our side of the fence now and you can't ever go back.' As I returned to my office I had one unwavering thought: anyone trying to challenge my authority would receive very short shrift. If it came to a battle of wills there could only ever be one winner, and that was going to be me.

The Technical Department encompassed several drawing offices under the control of the Technical Director, Stewart Tennant, a dour Scot who had spent all of his working life in various shipyards until finally settling in Belfast. The operational control, however, lay in the very capable hands of William (Billy) Harrison, the Chief Technical Manager, who had spent all his career at Harland & Wolff. He was now, at almost sixty years of age, one of the most experienced and capable Naval Architects in the business. Noted for his acerbic wit and biting put-downs, he had nevertheless earned the genuine respect and admiration of his contemporaries. Not one to suffer fools gladly, he had little time for people who sought the easy ride or who failed to perform their duties in the manner he expected of them.

He had a habit of making lightning, unannounced visits into the various drawing offices, his unerring eye for trouble having earned him the affectionate nickname of 'Old Bald Eagle', in apparent allusion to his award of an OBE some years before. An example of his knack for spotting an unfortunate individual came during a particularly warm summer day in the 'Glass House', a drawing office with a vaulted glass roof which resulted in it being unbearably hot in sunny conditions. As luck would have it Harrison arrived, unannounced as usual, to inspect the work in progress, and from the far side of the office spotted a draughtsman who had fallen asleep at his drawing board, obviously a victim of the oppressive heat. The Chief Draughtsman, realising that Harrison had seen this unfortunate individual, quickly issued instructions that he should be immediately woken up. 'No, don't wake him,' said Harrison, 'for while he sleeps he still has a job,' and with that he turned and left the office, leaving a furious and exceedingly embarrassed Chief Draughtsman in his wake. What he didn't see, however, was the slight smile that played about Billy Harrison's lips as we left the office together. It had been a good day, he had added another scalp to his belt and given a rather sleepy draughtsman one hell of a fright, not to mention a rather rude awakening from his boss.

During this time Harland & Wolff began to undergo a drastic metamorphosis which would have major repercussions for the future of the company. For many years the company had been losing money and had had to be rescued by massive cash injections from the Northern Ireland Government. Obviously such a situation could not be allowed to continue indefinitely, and so it was decided that the old board of the company had outlived its usefulness and had to be replaced. The United Kingdom Government, now the major shareholder in the company, decided that new and fresh ideas were needed to revitalise the company and looked to foreign shipyards, primarily in Scandinavia, for the expertise they needed to regenerate the ailing fortunes of the shipyard.

Unfortunately, this merely resulted in a huge influx of so-called experts and consultants, whose sole objective was to make as much money for themselves as quickly as they could, all the while giving the impression of working hard to modernise the company. It rapidly became obvious to all of us that a bunch of individuals who had absolutely no commitment or obligation to the company, and even less to Northern Ireland, had been foisted upon us. With frightening speed an air of demoralisation and dissension spread through the company, as all around us departments were shut down or amalgamated with others. Out of the blue we were being told that our ideas and methods were antiquated and that we had simply lost the ability to build ships efficiently and economically.

Highly qualified Naval Architects and Marine Engineers, who possessed a lifetime of experience, found themselves ignored as a host of foreign executives, mainly from Scandinavia, abruptly descended upon us. Sadly, in many cases these so-called experts proved to be anything but, and in the long run their interference effectively caused a massive haemorrhage within the company. The best of our home-grown talent resigned or retired in disgust at the developments taking place before them.

I was fortunate enough, or unfortunate enough, depending on your point of view, to experience this insane behaviour at first-hand when I sat in on an interview for a new Head of Design. This job was concerned specifically with the heating and ventilation systems which would be installed aboard the vessels we were to build. For over thirty years this area had been under the direction of an extremely competent engineer called Basil Lester, who had successfully designed the systems installed in over 140 ships. Despite this successful record, our new breed of consultants decreed that an HVAC (heating, ventilation and air conditioning) specialist was now required to oversee this area of operations. To add insult to injury, it was decided that Basil should form part of the interview panel. However, as it would turn out, this would prove to be a rather explosive experience for all concerned, especially for the interviewee.

The interview began well enough with the candidate, who happened to be Danish (in common with almost all of our new arrivals), giving a brief outline of his CV. A few routine questions followed, such as why he had a desire to live in Northern Ireland and his various hobbies and interests. Up to this point Basil had said nothing. Finally he indicated he had a few questions of his own to put to the candidate. 'Tell me,' he said, 'you didn't mention the names of any ships you have designed systems for, could you tell us some of them please.' 'Sorry,' came the reply, 'I haven't actually worked on any ships before.' 'OK then tell us what oil rigs you have designed systems for,' Basil asked. 'Again that is not an area I am familiar with,' came the reply. 'Right then,' said Basil, becoming visibly exasperated at the lack of information, 'I'll make it simple for you. What marine installations have you been involved with?' 'Oh this will be my first. I've never worked in a marine environment before this,' came the astonishing reply. A stunned silence enveloped the room at this startling revelation, and it was some moments before anyone spoke. Of course it simply had to be Basil, the scent of vindication in his nostrils. 'Not much fuckin' use then are you?' he snarled as he stood up to leave. Suffice to say the candidate was duly appointed as Head of HVAC design. He lasted about six months before resigning after single-handedly managing to completely devastate the morale and capability of his department. Of course it wasn't all gloom and doom; with the benefit of his experience Basil thankfully managed to repair almost all of the damage, and then as a final act of revenge he himself resigned from the company having proved his point in the most conclusive manner he could.

The changes taking place in the company were not confined simply to the Operational Systems and Personnel Departments. The image and logo of the company became the next target for a radical make-over. Ever since the company was founded in 1861 the company flag had been red, blue and yellow quarters with the H&W initials in black on a diamond device in the centre of the flag. After months of consideration by image consultants costing several thousand pounds, the new corporate flag was revealed to an expectant workforce, and what a disappointment it turned out to be. The much-anticipated 'new and vibrant' image that had been promised turned out to be nothing more glamorous than a plain yellow flag with the letters H&W in black in the centre.

It rapidly became clear to almost everyone involved in the management of the company that change was being implemented simply for the sake of change, and those changes that were made did nothing to provide the company with the fresh impetus it required. The next area to feel the impact of this lust was the main entrance and reception area, which up until now had been a showpiece of Victorian craftsmanship. This magnificent hallway was panelled in mahogany, teak-polished to perfection and inlaid with ornate carvings etched out in gold leaf. The entrance foyer was built from the finest Italian marble and inlaid throughout with an ink-black Onyx H&W motif.

The immediate impression on first entering this area was one of timeless elegance and grace. One instantly thought that here was a company that valued, cherished and maintained its traditional standards of quality and worked hard to maintain its good reputation. That was until the revamp inflicted upon it by the image consultants. Gone was the rich, deep-pile Wilton carpet, swept away was the wonderful wood-panelling, while the stunning oil paintings that had adorned the walls were lost to the company forever. In their place was a mish-mash of grey flock wallpaper and Formica-faced panels, which for all the world looked like some downmarket cafeteria or sixties milk bar. However, it was the carpet that really stood out. This was a specially manufactured concoction in an extremely light, two-tone grey colour with the H&W logo interwoven through the fabric in brilliant white, it was reported to have cost no less than £250,000.

Notwithstanding the expense, it must be acknowledged that the carpet was indeed stunning and most impressive in design, nonetheless it was completely impractical for everyday use in such a busy area. This was the main thoroughfare for all visitors to the company as well as the route for the various office staff to go about their business, and within the space of a few days the carpet would begin to display signs of dirt and grime from the thousands of feet that had walked over it. Clearly, the condition of the carpet would rapidly deteriorate unless steps were taken to limit the amount of use it was receiving, and to this end the various trade union representatives were called to a meeting with the Personnel Director to discuss the issue. Completely disregarding the fact that for over 140 years staff arriving for work had, by tradition, always used the main entrance to the company, he bluntly demanded that in future all staff would be required to use the rear entrance at all times. Furthermore, all staff would in future avoid using the main lobby to access other areas of the building and instead use the back corridors and fire escapes when going to another office or department. In conclusion, the Personnel Director announced, rather precipitately, that while he had afforded the representatives of the various trade unions the courtesy of this meeting to advise them of the company's demands, the substance of this diktat was not open to debate or discussion.

Obviously the announcement of such an uncompromising position came as something of a shock to those present, and for a moment they sat in stunned silence, until eventually the senior representative asked if he may at the very least be permitted to ask a question. Receiving agreement that this would be acceptable and speaking in an unusually quiet voice, he politely asked, 'Why are we being forced to accept this change to our terms and conditions of employment?'

Rolling his eyes heavenwards in an exaggerated show of impatience, the Personnel Director responded with just a hint of sarcasm, 'Because we have a new and very expensive carpet in the main foyer and we want to keep people from walking on it.' 'In that case why didn't you stick it on the fucking ceiling then?' came the blunt retort, adding for good measure, 'The staff will use the entrance they have traditionally used or you will have a strike on your hands,' and with that he abruptly rose to his feet and stormed out of the room. Over the coming weeks the staff carried on much as usual, although, if truth be told, many found excuses to make their way across the foyer even more regularly than they had in the past. This meant that the carpet received much more traffic than would have been normal, and as a consequence suffered much greater wear and tear than expected.

Just as everyone had forecast, the carpet proved to be a disastrous idea and was proved to be totally unsuitable for use in such a busy area, becoming filthy and shabby in just a few weeks. Various solutions were adopted to try and improve matters, but all to no avail, and in fact they served only to add to the embarrassment of all those who had been involved in its conception. Perhaps the whole business may best be summed-up by the words of a visiting dignitary, who remarked that the carpet looked like it had been designed by someone with 'more money than bloody sense'. He had no idea of just how right he was.

It would of course be unfair to say that all the disasters which befell the company during this period of rapid change could be laid at the door of the 'foreign legion'. Although this group were rapidly assuming positions of authority throughout the company, we were quite capable of creating spectacular disasters all of our own. One such incident started innocently enough with the arrival of a fishing vessel, the MV *Veronica*, for some minor repairs to its electrical generator.

The *Veronica* was the mainstay of the Republic of Ireland's fishing industry, and was in effect a floating factory which could clean, pack and freeze all the fish caught by the many trawlers which made up the Republic's fishing fleet. Such was her importance to that industry that she was to be maintained in permanently pristine condition, with no expense spared on any necessary repair or maintenance. Unfortunately, it was this high degree of care which would prove to be its Achilles heel. Repairs had been going well and the new generator was being installed without any undue difficulty, nevertheless, because of the importance of the vessel we were advised that the Irish Fisheries Minister wished to pay a courtesy visit to Harland & Wolff. This was intended as an opportunity to inspect the vessel and the ongoing repairs.

This news was enough to persuade the vessel's master to have a few minor dents and scratches evident on the vessel's hull removed, again a very simple job but one which would greatly enhance the ship's appearance. The work to remove these dents would entail heating up the surrounding metal until it was red-hot and then literally hammering out the dent prior to repainting the area. In the case of the repair operation on the *Veronica*, this would also involve the removal of some of the wood and polystyrene insulation in the fish processing area to permit access to the damaged areas.

Unfortunately, some of these dents extended into other areas separated by internal bulkheads or walls. This made the removal of sufficient insulation difficult as it was impossible to see what lay on the other side of the bulkhead. The outworker was compelled to rely purely on measurement of the area to ensure that enough material had been removed prior to commencing heating operations.

Work had just commenced on heating the hull in the fish packing room when reports of smoke began to arrive on the bridge of the vessel. On investigation it quickly became evident that a fierce fire was burning among the stacks of cardboard fish boxes, which had been ignited by burning insulation from the bulkhead above. The fire quickly spread through the storage area and was an inferno by the time the fire brigade arrived some five minutes later. Although they immediately set about attempting to tackle the blaze the task was anything but straightforward, as one cannot simply pump thousands of gallons of water into a floating ship without causing it to have serious stability problems.

The fire brigade faced this imponderable conundrum: how to fight an extremely fierce fire in a very enclosed space without the benefit of the unlimited use of water? While frantic efforts continued in order to save the vessel from further damage, the Irish Fisheries Minister, together with the *Veronica*'s master and our Ship Repair Director, had been enjoying a convivial lunch at a local hotel and were journeying back to Harland & Wolff. As they approached, a thick plume of smoke was spotted rising high into the sky over Belfast. In words that were to prove strangely prophetic, the *Veronica*'s master jokingly remarked, 'I hope that's not my ship that's on fire.' Their amusement very quickly turned to horror when it suddenly became apparent that it was indeed the *Veronica* which was on fire, with large sheets of flame leaping high into the air from her now red-hot and blistering decks. As the party arrived back alongside the stricken vessel, their mood became one of sombre resignation as it soon became obvious they were witnessing nothing short of a disaster of monumental proportions. Everyone present at this unfolding scene of devastation stood around in a rather sheepish silence, watching helplessly as the vessel became ever more gutted by the raging inferno consuming everything before it. The heat from the smouldering deck was so intense that the firemen were forced to abandon their efforts to contain the blaze, as the soles of their rubber boots were beginning to melt and stick to the roasting-hot steel deck plates.

All that afternoon and late into the evening, strenuous efforts were made by the fire brigade to quell the blaze. These gallant efforts were particularly laudable considering the obvious handicaps of difficulty of access and the increasingly precarious condition of the vessel. Eventually, several hours later, the fire was finally brought under control, but not without serious consideration having been given to simply towing the stricken vessel out into the deep waters of Belfast Lough and allowing it to sink under its own weight. After a further two days, the hulk of the *Veronica* had cooled sufficiently to allow damage assessors to board the vessel and carry out a close inspection of the hull and machinery.

The survey revealed that the damage sustained in the fire had proved so extensive that there was no alternative but to declare the vessel a constructive total loss, and she was consequently sent for scrap a few months later. Of more importance than the actual damage caused to the vessel was the disastrous impact and inconvenience the loss of the *Veronica* would inflict on the Irish fishing industry. The Irish Government found themselves, at very short notice, having to scour the world in an effort to locate a suitable replacement vessel for immediate charter until the *Veronica* could be replaced. Despite this catastrophic blow to the industry, perhaps the greatest damage of all was that sustained by Harland & Wolff to its reputation, and it would be many years indeed before the loss of face experienced by all those involved in this incident would subside. While the *Veronica* debacle was certainly a disaster of monumental proportions, it was nevertheless a complete accident rather than an act of sheer incompetence or carelessness, unlike that which befell another fishing vessel that had the misfortune to arrive in Harland & Wolff to undergo some minor repairs.

From the outset it has to be said that in this incident the vessel in question was an unofficial visitor to the company. Put another way it was to be a 'homer', a favour being done by a shipyard manager for one of his friends. On the day in question, the little wooden trawler arrived at the quayside ready for work to commence, including some minor engine repairs and the repainting of the underwater hull. This would, under normal circumstances, necessitate the dry-docking of the vessel. However, as this is a rather expensive and time-consuming process, requiring that prior notice be given to the Harbour Commissioners together with the advance payment of considerable docking fees, it was decided to adopt a more unorthodox method to remove the vessel from the water. It is a common assumption that Harland & Wolff are the owners of the dry-docks within the boundaries of the shipyard. This is incorrect, as in point of fact they are the property of the Harbour Commissioners, and as such are simply leased to Harland & Wolff as and when they are required. Furthermore, as the dry-docks available to Harland & Wolff are of massive proportions, they are intended for much larger vessels than a tiny trawler, and it was decided to simply lift the vessel out of the water onto the quayside by means of a mobile crane.

Slings or cradles were duly placed under the trawler, and the lift commenced without any hint of the catastrophe that was about to strike with such devastating effect. The arm of the mobile crane reached out from the quayside and over the trawler as it slowly began to lift the small vessel out of the water and high enough into the air to allow it to swing clear of the side of the jetty. The initial stage of the lift had been completed, with the little vessel now high in the air as the crane began its traverse landwards, when suddenly a horrible metallic screeching noise was heard from the winch gear on the crane. Smoke began to pour from the cable drum as the strain on the mechanism rapidly reached, and then exceeded, its safe operating limit. To his horror, the crane driver swiftly realised that he was now in serious difficulty, and in a frantic attempt to recover the situation began to traverse the crane towards the quayside as fast as he could. Unfortunately, this only had the effect of further destabilising the crane and increasing the already critical load on the lifting cables.

With a resounding bang like a gunshot firing, the lifting cables snapped apart like dry twigs as they gave up the unequal struggle to support the load. This parted the little trawler from the crane slings and it came crashing down, smashing onto the quay below with a rumble like thunder as it disappeared into a cloud of dust and smoke.

As we stood there in shocked silence, unable to quite comprehend what we had just witnessed, the cloud of dust slowly began to clear to reveal that nothing more remained of the little trawler than a large pile of smashed timber and glass. From somewhere just behind me came a lone voice which cut like a knife through the stunned silence. 'Fuck me, I'd like to see the joiner who puts that back together again.'

Swiftly the humour of the situation overcame our astonishment and we began to laugh, more from relief that nobody had been hurt rather than any actual humour at what had just happened. For my own part I was only too relieved that I was not going to be the poor sod who had to tell the trawler's owner that his pride and joy was now nothing more than a pile of matchwood. In the end, Harland & Wolff very generously accepted full responsibility for the destruction of the trawler, even though the vessel should never have been in the yard at all, and agreed a suitable compensation sum with the owner. In a comparable company such gaffes would, in all probability, have spelt the end of the career of the manager involved. However, in Harland & Wolff making drastic errors of judgement could be advantageous. One particular case which illustrates this point is that of a senior executive who was known for his fiery temper and colourful language. In the mid-1980s the company negotiated a cooperation agreement with the Kawasaki shipyard in Japan, whose methods and philosophy were regarded enviously as the ideal model upon which to base the regeneration of Harland & Wolff. When this manager was appointed as the project liaison director, the hoped-for progress and cooperation towards this regeneration goal suffered a rapid and acrimonious stalling when, during an alcohol-fuelled dinner party to welcome the visiting Japanese consultants, it was widely reported that he referred to them as 'slitty-eyed bastards who could teach us fuck all about shipbuilding'.

Despite the best efforts of Harland & Wolff's senior executives and much diplomatic oil being poured on the troubled waters, the relationship between the two companies was never quite the same again. The proposed integration project simply ran out of steam and, much to everyone's relief, eventually fizzled out. Working practices in the shipyard very quickly returned to pretty much what they had always been as we waited for the inevitable next 'brilliant wheeze' to be inflicted upon us.

Regrettably, by this time the general workforce had become so demoralised that the majority really didn't care about the future of the company anymore. It seemed that no sooner had we reorganised to facilitate the introduction of some new methodology than it was time to do it all over again. As a means of creating a dispirited and discontented workforce, the continual reorganisation of a company structure takes some beating. It gives ample opportunities for wasting time while at the same time presenting the illusion of making progress. As future developments would reveal, this systematic and calculated demoralisation of the workforce was a deliberate manoeuvre on the part of senior management, and was intended to achieve quite a sinister purpose.

Chapter Seven

As my career in Harland & Wolff progressed, I gradually began to take on an increasingly diverse range of tasks in my role as Technical Department administrator and, just two short years after my return to the department, I received a promotion to assistant manager grade. This elevation in my status had not been entirely unexpected as, for several months previously, I had been undertaking a much wider range of duties and responsibilities than my predecessor. Naturally I was delighted that my efforts and abilities had been recognised, and I thoroughly relished the opportunities I had been presented with to further develop my spheres of responsibility and advance my career within the company as far as possible.

I had achieved the distinction of being the first person in my position to get a foot on the first rung of the management ladder. However, like all things in life it had its advantages and disadvantages. I can vividly recall the words the general manager used when first telling me of my promotion: 'I suppose you realise there is no going back, you're one of the enemy now.' I understood he was making a joke to illustrate a very important point; I had gone from being just another 'one of the boys', I had crossed over that invisible line and joined 'the management'. Things would never be the same again – my former colleagues were now my staff and had to obey my instructions and directions. As I contemplated the full meaning of these words, a brief chill gripped my heart and a shiver ran down my spine. Deep inside I knew I hadn't changed as a person, but to do my job effectively I realised I now needed to ensure that everything I did from that moment on would be seen as fair and balanced. Many of my staff were also personal friends, and I was very alert to the possibility that this could be a disadvantage in many ways. I would need to be extremely careful not to allow any favouritism to colour my judgement.

As it was I needn't have worried, as the general consensus of opinion amongst the staff was one of good wishes and congratulations. For the first time – well, for as long as I could remember at least – I began to look forward to coming into work each morning. I began to experience a strange kind of euphoria, knowing that to all intents and purposes I now had a roving commission in which I could make my own operational decisions and discover the joys and pitfalls of running my own department. Of course I also had lots of fun in discovering some of the less obvious benefits of becoming a member, albeit a junior one, of the management team, and the perks that came with the territory. The company had maintained an arcane structure in the dining arrangements it provided for its workforce. These comprised three distinct levels and were collectively known as the 'troughs'. Directors and senior managers were allocated the 'Golden Trough' and enjoyed a rather eclectic menu and fine wine with their lunch. Middle and junior management were allocated the 'Silver Trough', where waitress and silver service was provided. However, wine was most definitely prohibited. The fare on offer was the same as that provided in the 'Trough', or works canteen.

The standard of meals provided to the works was quite high and a choice of main course was always offered, although the ubiquitous chips could always be found. These dining facilities were especially welcome during the winter period, as the opportunity to enjoy a hot meal in warm surroundings was eagerly accepted. Certainly, dining in the 'Trough' could be a hazardous occupation, as staff and works' employees joined in what, at times, appeared to be apparently endless queues followed by an unseemly scramble to find a seat while attempting to balance your meal on a tray. On occasion, the effort to maintain the equilibrium between hand and tray ended in abject failure, resulting in an almighty crash as the tray and its contents plunged to the floor. To the abject embarrassment of the hapless individual concerned, this immediately resulted in a cry of 'A big hand for the juggler' emanating from several sections of the room.

Now elevated to the Silver Trough, I could enjoy the luxury of waitress service, starched table linen and silver cutlery, and while only water or juice were available to drink, it was served in the very best crystal glassware. Despite, or perhaps because, of this apparent decadence, almost everyone aspired to reach the ultimate level of self-indulgence by gaining admission to the Directors and senior management dining room. The Golden Trough was the ultimate symbol of decadence and indulgence, a sure sign that one had 'arrived'. However, from my personal perspective I was content enough just to have made it this far, after all, a chip is still just a chip, no matter how fancy the surroundings.

One of my new responsibilities, a welcome diversion from my normal activities, was to look after and entertain visitors to the company who would be attending the naming or float-out of a completed vessel. On such occasions the vessel's owner would provide the company with a list of guests whom they had invited to the ceremony, and which the company secretary's office would then divide up into easily manageable groups. Each of these groups would be assigned to a particular manager, who would then have responsibility for ensuring their visit to the company went without a hitch and that they were adequately entertained during their stay. This usually involved organising trips to local places of interest or shopping excursions for the ladies, and usually joining them for dinner or drinks at their hotel in the evenings.

Mindful of the need to create a good impression of the company, perhaps the most important part of these duties was the actual meeting and greeting of your nominated party upon their arrival at the airport and then escorting them to their hotel. Usually such occasions presented no difficulty, and after introducing yourself to your party and presenting a brief outline of the planned events the guests were whisked away with the minimum of fuss. As an established routine it worked flawlessly, or rather it did, until the appearance of a rather large batch of visitors who arrived by a chartered private jet at Belfast International Airport. After much deliberation it was decided that because the party was so large, just over forty people and their assorted baggage, it would be impossible to utilise the usual fleet of limousines, and therefore it would be necessary to charter a luxury coach to provide the necessary transportation to their hotels.

Ulsterbus Ltd, who were the national transport company in Northern Ireland and had vast experience in such jobs, were contacted, and arrangements were quickly concluded for the hire of their newest and very best luxury coach complete with an experienced driver for the evening. Given the pedigree of the guests, nothing was to be left to chance. However, as events were to unfold, the choice of Ulsterbus to provide the transportation would prove to be the downfall of the carefully choreographed arrangements.

On the evening in question the assistant company secretary, the coach, and its accompanying driver were all ready at the airport entrance awaiting the arrival of the chartered jet and its passengers. The company had earlier arranged special permission with the airport authorities to park outside the main terminal exit, an area usually reserved for passenger service vehicles and taxis. All appeared to be going to plan as the aircraft duly arrived on schedule, the passengers quickly disembarked into the terminal VIP area and their baggage was swiftly collected and loaded aboard the waiting coach. After presenting a brief speech of welcome to Belfast, the assistant company secretary escorted the party of guests aboard the coach waiting to speed them on their way to the city. Unfortunately, what no one appreciated or anticipated at the time was that Ulsterbus also provided the normal bus service from Belfast International to Great Victoria Street coach station in the centre of Belfast. What's more, the chartered coach was adorned with its normal Ulsterbus company livery and had been parked at the usual airport bus stop.

All this was far from the assistant secretary's mind as the coach made its way out of the airport. Relieved that his pick-up had gone without any apparent problems, he busied himself by providing the guests with a brief commentary on the events planned for the next few days and pointed out the various places of interest they passed as the coach journeyed on its way towards the five-star Culloden Hotel situated on the outskirts of the city. All was progressing smoothly until the coach crossed over the Queens Bridge in the centre of Belfast and turned left onto the Sydenham by-pass which ran alongside the Harland & Wolff complex. The assistant secretary was astonished to see an elderly woman clutching a battered carrier bag make her way along the aisle of the coach towards him. 'Excuse me son,' she croaked, 'but is this bus not supposed to stop at the Europa?'

Named after what is widely believed to be the most bombed hotel in Europe (a legacy of our troubled history), the Europa is the name by which Great Victoria Street bus station is better known by the populace of Belfast. Forgetting his composure and the fact that the eyes of over forty VIPs were now fixed intently upon him, he hissed, 'Where the bloody hell did you come from, and how the fuck did you get on this bus?' It later transpired that the old lady had been at the airport to see her son off to London and, spotting the coach waiting at the bus stop, naturally assumed it was the bus to Belfast. Being rather small in stature she had boarded the coach unseen by anyone and settled herself down in a seat at the rear of the coach where she had promptly dozed off.

Unfortunately for the assistant secretary, she was now wide awake and began loudly demanding that she be taken to the bus station immediately. Brushing aside all attempts to placate her or explain the situation, she further added to the entertainment by taking occasional swipes at him with her umbrella. The party of visiting dignitaries thought the whole episode hilarious, and word of the incident quickly did the rounds of Harland & Wolff. As for the old lady, she remained with the party until they arrived at the Culloden Hotel, where she was treated to supper with her new found companions and provided with a taxi home at Harland & Wolff's expense. As for the assistant secretary, he became the unwilling recipient of the very first 'golden egg' award to be presented in the company for services to embarrassment above and beyond the call of duty.

It would perhaps be helpful if at this point I offer a few words of explanation regarding this award. The golden egg award was an idea stolen from a BBC light entertainment programme, whereby individuals who had made a very embarrassing mistake or been caught out in a humiliating situation were presented with a golden egg. This being Harland & Wolff, of course our version was made from solid steel and weighed almost a hundredweight! Sadly, despite our best efforts, we could not obtain any gold paint to complete the effect. However, as the company colours were now predominantly yellow anyway, paint of this colour was readily available. In preparation for its forthcoming fame, the steel egg was duly dispatched to the paint hall where it was to be shot-blasted and spray-painted a lurid yellow.

When it eventually returned from the painting process, everyone was highly amused to note that not only did it appear to have developed a somewhat jaundiced appearance, it had also acquired the embellishment of a magnificent and rather ornate fluted plinth, mounted atop a stepped base. Unfortunately, this additional adornment had added considerably to the overall weight of the piece, and it now required the services of two men and a fork-lift truck to move it anywhere. What had started out as a simple representation of an egg was now almost three feet in height and an awesome weight. Because of this we had no alternative other than to have it permanently installed in a corner of the general secretarial office, where the 'lucky' recipients of a golden egg were presented *to* their award rather than *with* it as under normal circumstances. To mark the occasion, however, winners were presented with a hard-boiled egg inscribed with their name and an award citation printed on vellum.

While golden eggs were awarded for dropping a spectacular clanger, a quite different accolade was eagerly sought by crews taking part in the sea trials of an almost completed vessel. Such trials usually lasted for a week, and competition was fierce among the engineering and design staff to achieve the record of spending the most time asleep in their bunk. While engaged on sea trials these individuals were on call at all times and, depending on prevailing circumstances or the nature of operations, could be on duty for anything over twenty-four hours at a stretch. The more experienced engineers and technicians had somehow developed an uncanny knack of anticipating when a difficult situation might possibly occur, and could therefore usually manage to forestall any potential problems.

As a result the most astute engineers were able to enjoy a relatively trouble-free trip, and could focus their energies on mounting a challenge for the prestigious 'golden blanket' award for the most time spent supine in their bunks. The most frequent recipient of this honour was the engineer responsible for the design and installation of the propulsion and rudder systems used by the various vessels. Hugh Gilmour was a veritable genius in this field and had no equal throughout Harland & Wolff. An engineer of the old school, he shunned the use of computers, preferring to perform all his design calculations with pen and paper, or as he would often describe it, 'on the back of a fag packet'.

Hugh had become a legend throughout the company for his unrivalled success in the golden blanket competition; such was his confidence that he never departed on sea trials without a vast stack of magazines and books to while away the hours. It is a tribute to his expertise that in over sixty vessels for which Hugh had propulsion systems responsibility, none suffered any major breakdown or excess vibration. His legend was further enhanced by an incident involving a rather pernickety owner's representative. This incident occurred during a speed trial over the measured mile course just off Arran Island, or 'Paddy's milestone' as it is better known to seafarers. The incident revolved around the number of engine revolutions required to achieve the stipulated vessel speed through the water. On the case in question, the owner's engineering representative in attendance was demanding that the engine revolutions be increased fractionally in order to achieve one additional knot of speed.

This process had been going on all morning with the representative, much to Hugh's increasing frustration and impatience, demanding ever more precise measurements of the vessel speed in relation to engine revolutions. In exasperation Hugh demanded to know how much longer this unnecessary and time-consuming exercise would continue, especially as the vessel had easily reached the contractual and designed performance criteria. 'Until I am satisfied,' came the blunt response, which only served to infuriate Hugh even more. It wasn't long before yet another speed change was ordered. 'Increase revolutions by 2 per cent and calculate estimated as opposed to actual vessel speed, and report same to me.' The imperious tone used to issue this order proved to be the final straw for Hugh, and, pressing his nose into the face of the owner's representative, he demanded, 'What bloody speed and revs is it you are wanting?' 'I want the engine evolutions steady at 75 and the speed to be constant at 17 knots, do you think you can manage that?' With hindsight it would have been better if the owner's representative hadn't added that somewhat unnecessary final comment, or what followed next certainly could have been avoided.

With the air of a man possessed, Hugh marched across the engine room towards the main engine control panel with its multitude of dials and gauges. Removing his boot, Hugh selected both the revolution counter and vessel speed indicators and then deliberately smashed the glass on each with the heel of his boot. He then grasped the indicator needles and with a swift twist of his wrist bent them until each pointed to the requested position. 'Satisfied now?' snarled Hugh, 'And you can shove yer clipboard up yer arse as well you oul get.' With that Hugh retired to his bunk for the rest of the day, where none of us had any intention whatsoever of disturbing him.

Obviously there were repercussions over the incident, but in the main everyone considered that the owner's representative had received his just deserts. In actual fact, the owner's marine superintendent revealed that the engineer was universally disliked by his colleagues, and he was delighted that the incident gave him the perfect excuse to have him recalled to their head office in England.

The opportunity to participate in the sea trials of any vessel was always highly prized, not least because of the chance to earn vast amounts of overtime pay. Living cheek by jowl for almost two weeks, often among strangers, did, at times, produce some amusing incidents. The P&O liner *Canberra* had successfully completed the first series of builders' trials, where the vessel and its systems were tested to ensure they were operating satisfactorily and in accordance with the contract specification. The next stage was the owner's acceptance trials when, if everything was on the button, the vessel would be accepted by its owner as completed. P&O had decided that during this second series of sea trials for *Canberra*, quite apart from the normal familiarisation procedures for the engineering officers, it would be a useful training exercise for the stewards to practise their skills at serving meals in the dining room. To this end the Harland & Wolff complement on board were to act as passengers, with certain individuals being encouraged to play the role of a particularly awkward customer. To keep the training as realistic as possible in gauging how well they handled an awkward situation, the stewards were not told about this subterfuge. However, they were told that all complaints were to be treated seriously and to regard the shipyard personnel as genuine fare-paying passengers.

Things had been progressing well in the dining room and the meals were being prepared and served from the galley with the minimum of fuss. As always aboard cruise liners, a wide choice of food was available, and the Harland & Wolff contingent were doing their best to sample every delicacy on offer. One evening smoked salmon was featured on the menu and one of the fitters, despite never having heard of it, but being very partial to tinned salmon, thought it sounded ideal. The steward duly took his order and returned a few minutes later with the requested dish, which he served with his usual aplomb, wishing the now rather surprised fitter *bon appetit*.

'Ah excuse me mate,' came the response, 'but is there no chips with this?' At first the steward thought he was about to become the victim of a practical joke, chips with a smoked salmon starter indeed! But on returning to the table he rapidly realised his customer was quite serious in his comment. Overcoming his initial surprise, the steward quickly regained his composure and wrongly assumed that this must be a test of his abilities in dealing with an awkward passenger, especially as he noticed the chief steward watching him intently from a corner of the dining saloon. 'Certainly sir,' he replied with a beaming smile, 'I will just be a few moments, my sincere apologies for the delay.' With that he disappeared into the galley, returning a few minutes later with a steaming plate of freshly cooked chips. 'I trust everything is to your satisfaction sir?' he enquired politely. 'No it bloody well isn't,' came the abrupt response. 'The fish is cold and the portion's not very big is it?'

Meals continued to be problematic, especially on cargo vessels and even more so on oil tankers, where the officers' quarters are situated in a mid-ship deck house while the crew quarters and the galley are located at the stern. I vividly recall one very blustery day when a young officer cadet selected a delicious-looking green salad for his lunch, but instead of eating with us in the mess room he opted to return with it to his cabin. On oil tankers the various accommodation areas are connected by a walkway built over the assorted pipes and valves that occupy the main deck, and while at sea this walkway can become very exposed in stormy conditions. The young cadet left the shelter of the galley and proceeded along the walkway in the teeth of a force eight gale towards the accommodation area some 150 metres away. As he battled his way forward, the swirling wind whipped pieces of his salad lunch high into the air until he arrived at his cabin, windswept and exhausted, with just a solitary piece of tomato remaining on his plate. He didn't return to the galley for another helping, I can only assume that he had had enough embarrassment for one day.

While I was definitely enjoying the freedom and privileges my position in the company afforded me, and was gaining in self-confidence as I picked-up more experience, my immediate future and that of the company was anything but secure. By the beginning of the 1980s, the workforce had endured almost ten years of uncertainty and upheaval in their working conditions, which had only served to produce a totally disaffected and disheartened labour force. A succession of Chairmen and Chief Executives came and went, ranging from several Swedish and Danish accountants to the local founder of a company of estate agents. By the time of this final appointment, a popular myth had gained hold among the incredulous workforce that he had been appointed simply in order to obtain the best price possible for any sale of the land and buildings. It was in this atmosphere of despondency that the first real glimmer of hope began to appear.

The company had been without a Chairman or Chief Executive for several months, nor did there appear to be any sign of these posts being filled in the near future. Given our past record, many high-flying executives would doubtless view the leadership of Harland & Wolff as being a poisoned chalice and the likely death knell for their careers. During the run-up to Christmas, with everybody aware of the possibility of closure should this dreadful uncertainty remain unresolved, it was to be expected that ever more desperate rumours would begin to circulate throughout the company. The main one of these was the suggestion that the Government was about to finally pull the plug on the whole shipbuilding operation. It was in the midst of all this gloom that a buzz of excitement suddenly began to flow through the company from top to bottom. Quickly the news spread: John Parker was coming back! If this was true it was the best possible news for the survival of Harland & Wolff.

John Parker was the archetypal 'local boy made good', however more importantly he was a Harland & Wolff man to the core. Supremely intelligent with a distinct flair for the intricacies of mathematical computation in theoretical ship design, his prodigious talent was quickly recognised and he rapidly progressed through the ranks of the drawing office. He was promoted from apprentice draughtsman to become one of the youngest Naval Architects in the history of the shipyard. A gifted and highly innovative ship designer, he had rapidly established a formidable reputation among his colleagues for his uncompromising dedication to the pursuit of excellence in ship design. This was a dedication which would lead to him being appointed Chief Naval Architect, and also head of the Design Department at the astonishingly early age of just thirty-two. Some argued this was an achievement which surpassed the accomplishments of perhaps the most famous ship designer in the long history of Harland & Wolff, Thomas Andrews, designer of the RMS *Titanic*.

I first met John Parker when he was a junior draughtsman, and found him to be one of the most approachable and friendly individuals I had ever met. Regardless of my lowly status as office message boy, he was unfailingly polite, never failing to say 'thank you' when I returned from the canteen with his snack or drink. Even at that early stage, everyone had recognised that here was an exceptional young man who was destined to go far, and consequently it was no surprise to see him attain the position he did so early in his career. Unfortunately for Harland & Wolff, his incisive, pioneering approach to the intricacies of ship design and hull form rapidly brought his remarkable abilities to the attention of other shipyards, and one day he inevitably received an offer he found impossible to resist.

British Shipbuilders, the nationalised shipbuilding industry on the British mainland, had been in the doldrums for several years, afflicted mainly by the same problems as Harland & Wolff, only on a much larger scale. The Government, deeply concerned at the vast sums of money they were continually having to provide in support of this ailing industry, were determined to find someone who they considered had the ability to reverse this tide of misfortune. They were looking for someone to rebuild a business that was, by this time, considered to be nothing more than an unacceptable drain on the public purse. After several months of intensive research they eventually identified just such a person in John Parker, and immediately offered him the position of Deputy Head of British Shipbuilding. The appointment proved to be an astute choice, as within a few years massive improvements in efficiency and productivity were evident right across the board. An innovative series of vessels were added to the design portfolio, such as the SD 14 and SD 15 standard dry cargo vessels, which became some of the most successful vessel designs ever produced, and rivalled the Second World War Liberty ship design in numbers produced.

Now, in November 1982, it appeared that the man who had almost single-handedly rescued British Shipbuilders from the point of extinction was about to attempt to do the same thing for Harland & Wolff. The task would be a

Herculean one to attempt, even for Parker, however he had one very distinct advantage over his immediate predecessors in that he was a local boy who had a love for, and more importantly a sense of loyalty to, the company.

For too many years Harland & Wolff had been under the leadership of individuals who had no particular affinity with the company, much less Northern Ireland. Regarded in the main as 'carpetbaggers', they had been content to accept vastly inflated salaries while seeking to exploit their personal position. Scandalous incidents of blatant exploitation were evident on an almost daily basis, which left the workforce increasingly outraged and despondent. One particularly appalling example of this duplicity came to light from the Annual Accounts of the company, where it was revealed that the current Chairman of Harland & Wolff was also the Chairman and principal owner of a marine consultancy company, and that this company was providing several executive staff to Harland & Wolff. In point of fact, this individual had used his consultancy company to simply hire himself and several more of his employees out to Harland & Wolff, while enjoying the benefits of collecting a large consultancy fee on top of the negotiated salary for each executive.

To add insult to injury, each member of this 'foreign legion' was accommodated in the very best hotels and provided with lavish expense accounts, not to mention first-class flights home to Scandinavia each weekend. Given such disreputable activities it is little wonder that the local management and employees were demoralised, expectations for their immediate future were being lowered almost daily. No one could understand why central Government, or indeed the local administration, such as it was, seemingly turned a blind eye to such disgraceful conduct. Of course we all had our suspicions, but proof of complicity in such impropriety was another thing altogether.

It was into such a poisoned atmosphere that John Parker returned to take the helm at Harland & Wolff, and as was typical of the man he immediately set about winning the confidence of the workforce by instituting a rolling programme whereby he would personally meet every employee within one month of his return to the company. Once again, all of us who had known him previously would be astounded by his phenomenal memory as he unfailingly remembered each one of our names, and it is true to say that each of us who left those meetings had a renewed sense of purpose and confidence. Unfortunately, and unbeknown to us at the time, we had not completely rid ourselves of the scourge of foreign influence within the company. A few months later the Government, for reasons that made sense only to them, insisted on the appointment of yet another foreign consultant.

The arrival of Per Nielsen from Denmark was greeted with some scepticism, if not cynicism, by those unfortunate enough to have experienced his complete lack of personality at first hand. From the outset it was abundantly clear that he had very little regard for Harland & Wolff, and even less for Northern Ireland.

The initial unfavourable impression that we were being saddled with yet another foreign 'carpetbagger', was further reinforced by the discovery that his vastly inflated salary was to be paid directly into an off-shore trust based in the Channel Islands. Despite the obvious disquiet this revelation caused among the company management, and the lack of commitment it demonstrated towards his new position, the arrangements remained in place right up until his resignation many years later. With hindsight the arrival of Per Nielsen could certainly be regarded as one of the blackest days in the long history of Harland & Wolff.

His appointment would turn out to be the beginning of the end for the company, as his inconsistent decisions would eventually bring it to its knees. However, at the time all this was far from everyone's thoughts. We had just received what was perhaps the best Christmas present we could get that year. We were simply happy enough just to welcome back somebody that, at last, we knew we could trust with our future.

Chapter Eight

From a personal perspective, the very welcome return of John Parker to the running of the company had very little immediate impact on my day-to-day activities within the Technical Department. Indeed, by this time I had added another string to my bow as, almost imperceptibly, I began to assume *de facto* responsibility for the company archives.

One of my routine tasks within the Technical Department was to provide copies of construction drawings for vessels previously built by the company. These requests came from a number of sources, but in the main they occurred when a vessel was sold or was undergoing repair in another shipyard. This activity had made me aware of the vast amount of technical information the company had at its disposal, data that would be an invaluable resource to students of naval architecture as well as anyone interested in the history and development of shipbuilding. This vast collection of material, accumulated since the earliest days of Harland & Wolff, totalled somewhere in the region of two million individual drawings and plans, technical specification manuals including trim and stability data, together with hundreds of thousands of irreplaceable photographs.

Unfortunately, it quickly became clear that this unique anthology, chronicling the history of one of the greatest shipbuilding yards in the world, was being badly neglected. Locked away in strong rooms and drawing stores across the shipyard, this priceless and irreplaceable asset had been allowed to simply languish, forgotten and disregarded, as it slowly decayed due to age and neglect. I understood and appreciated from previous experience that this wealth of knowledge could be utilised as a valuable research tool for the various museums and ship societies throughout the world and, with careful marketing, it could be an invaluable asset to the company. Harland & Wolff frequently received requests for this material from the owners of ships built by the company or other shipyards, as the repair of such vessels required copies of various construction drawings. While servicing such requests did provide a source of income, the amount realised in many cases barely covered the administrative expenses involved in providing the information. The task of searching for and identifying the correct drawings was made more difficult and time-consuming for the clerical staff as no comprehensive records for the drawings existed. In order to make the whole operation cost-effective, and to properly appreciate the significance of the resource the company had at its disposal, I understood that the first task would be to have the archives accurately indexed with all the major drawings centralised in one location. Achieving this apparently simple objective would see the current operational costs fall dramatically, and go a long way to making the whole process at least cost-effective, if not a vastly more profitable exercise.

With all this in mind I put together a draft proposal outlining my suggestions to the Chief Technical Manager for his consideration. I half-expected my proposal to receive a lukewarm reception. However, much to my surprise and delight it was accepted and approved without reservation. As was common practice in the company at the time, even if only to show that the document had been read, any proposed new procedures would usually receive approval after at least some amendment or comment had been made on them. Unsure if this unusually smooth acceptance of my proposal was either good fortune or a poisoned chalice, I began the gradual transition into becoming the company archivist.

The logistics of reorganising the various drawing stores into one centralised facility were simple enough, and after only a few months the whole operation was running like a well-oiled machine. We received many requests for copies of archival drawings, which were usually processed within twenty-four hours of receipt. This tremendous improvement in service response time did not go unnoticed by several ship owners, and played no small part in giving an overall impression of improving efficiency within Harland & Wolff as a whole.

A further, but less quantifiable, benefit was the public relations value in being able to provide a service to the general public, in particular those with an interest in the RMS *Titanic*, perhaps the most famous vessel in history. The company had always been very reluctant to provide any technical information, or any details whatsoever, on this particular vessel. They preferred to reply to each request with the standard response 'The company are unable to assist you in obtaining the information you have requested'.

I had felt for some considerable time that by taking such an approach the company was creating the false impression that it had something to hide, and therefore I immediately set about changing this negative attitude by being more open and responsive in dealing with such enquiries. It appeared logical to me that the history and fate of the RMS *Titanic* should be one of immense interest to everyone from historians to ship enthusiasts right across the world, and by our refusal to openly address the issue the company had developed an unwelcome reputation for being obstructive. I therefore decided to redress the balance by introducing a more open and accommodating attitude to our historical legacy, in particular that of the RMS *Titanic*, and thus adopt a more cooperative manner in the way we handled such matters. Accordingly, one of my first duties was to organise a press release to the effect that Harland & Wolff would be willing to answer any and all questions put to it in regard to the RMS *Titanic*. However, even I was stunned and amazed at the overwhelming response we would receive to this new-found openness.

Over the course of the next few months the company received several hundred letters and cards, containing quite literally thousands of questions about the building of the *Titanic*, with almost all asking for copies of the construction drawings. Within a short period of time I found myself increasingly being put forward as the unofficial spokesman for Harland & Wolff on the history of the company, and in particular that of the RMS *Titanic*. I very quickly appreciated the tremendous benefit to be made by using the archive records to raise the profile of the company, and while it would certainly not lead directly to any new orders being placed with the company, it would serve to keep the name of Harland & Wolff to the forefront of maritime circles. Because of my ever-increasing profile as the point of contact for the company in dealing with its historical matters, I soon acquired the additional title of Archive Manager to add to my previous title. I admit that while I revelled in my new-found celebrity status and the rather grandiose title of Archive and Administration Manager, in all honesty I enjoyed the rise in salary that accompanied it even more.

While the success of this new venture had greatly increased the profile of the company and considerably improved our public relations image, not everyone was enamoured with my efforts, and it wasn't long before Per Nielsen and I had the first of the many confrontations we were to have over the coming years. The conflict between us had started innocently enough. However, the experience I gained from it taught me an invaluable lesson in self-preservation.

At this stage I was keen to consolidate and build on the successful start I had made on the opening-up of the company archives, as well as hoping to capitalise on the unique place Harland & Wolff occupied in the history of Northern Ireland. I now wanted to establish formal links with the Northern Ireland Tourist Board as a means of positioning the company on the international tourist scene. The company had a singular and incomparable connection to the RMS *Titanic*, and the ongoing interest in the history of the vessel became an obvious starting point for future cooperation. For several years the Belfast City Corporation had been working in collaboration with a local omnibus company to provide bus tours of the city. Included in this excursion was a short trip along the Queens Road which ran through the heart of the shipyard. However, and rather unfortunately for the paying customers, this arrangement had a major drawback in that the bus was confined to the public road. As a consequence, very little of the actual ships or their construction areas could be seen. This tantalising glimpse of what was a major area of interest only served to whet the appetite of the general public, who became increasingly frustrated at being unable to get a closer look at the marvels of engineering. Regrettably, because of the continuing levels of civil unrest throughout Northern Ireland at this time, even these limited tours had to eventually be abandoned for security reasons. However, I felt that properly organised parties could still be safely accommodated and also provided with a more informative and interesting view of our operations.

To this end I arranged a meeting with the company's Director of Corporate Affairs to discuss my ideas, and hopefully gain her approval for me to officially approach the tourist board and sound out their reaction to our proposals. The meeting went well and I was granted permission to begin informal discussions with the tourist board; unfortunately for me, as I would be painfully reminded by later events, I made the unwitting mistake of failing to get confirmation of this permission in writing. In the meantime, blissfully unaware of the storm that was about to break over my head, I commenced discussions with the head of the tourist board which were very positive and well received. The tourist board rapidly appreciated the obvious fillip the opening-up of Harland & Wolff as a visitor attraction could be to their own marketing strategy for Northern Ireland. This was a particularly big consideration in such difficult times, and they were therefore especially keen to assist us in any way they could by providing both financial and marketing support whenever necessary. The fact that a major facility like Harland & Wolff was willing to accept visitors to its works at such a difficult time for the city, presented a very welcome air of normality and served as a source of hope for the future. Certainly, the tourist board felt sufficiently encouraged by our positive attitude to consider issuing a formal press announcement when the negotiations were completed.

Over the next few weeks the discussions progressed to the stage where a formal Heads of Agreement was drafted and sent to the company for its approval or comments, and, as per the normal course of events, it duly arrived on Per Nielsen's desk whereupon it promptly exploded, or rather he did when he read it!

The first inkling I received of impending trouble was when I received an extremely terse telephone call from Nielsen's secretary ordering me to report to his office immediately. Innocently asking why he would wish to see me so urgently, I was informed that 'You will find out when you get here'. Somewhat surprised and indeed taken aback at such a brusque summons, I puzzled as to what I could have done to warrant such an abrupt order. Unconcerned, as I could not think of any reason to be apprehensive, I duly made my way to his office where

I found myself confronted by an almost apoplectic Nielsen. He immediately stormed from behind his desk to confront me as I entered the room. 'What the hell is this and what do you think you are doing???' he yelled, waving a sheaf of papers into my face. 'You are mad, mad, what are you thinking?' Taken aback by the ferocity of his attack, I could only stumble over my response by saying, 'Perhaps if you told me what you are talking about I might be able to understand what the problem is.' 'The problem is you, you are mad, mad, mad, and I think I will throw you out of the company!' he yelled, his voice now bordering on the hysterical. By this time my mind was struggling to comprehend the situation and I felt angry at what I dimly perceived to be some sort of ambush. Reasoning that if I really was in imminent danger of being sacked then I had nothing to lose, I followed the old adage that attack is the best form of defence. 'Listen!' I shouted, 'I don't have a bloody clue what you are yelling about, but one thing I do know is that I'm not fucking mad and neither am I scared of you, so either tell me what is wrong or shut up!' This rather unconventional approach to dealing with the Deputy Chief Executive appeared to have the desired effect, and he appeared to partially calm down, well at least enough to make it clear why he was so angry.

As he spoke it soon became apparent that he had been totally unaware of my discussions with the tourist board until the Heads of Agreement document had arrived on his desk. Furthermore, he was completely and implacably opposed to my ideas, and had overreacted in the manner he had when he finally discovered what had been going on. 'No one told me about this, why was I not informed?' he said, addressing his remark vaguely in my direction. It was at that point I made the mistake that would see us become implacable opponents from that moment on: 'Perhaps if you didn't shout so much people would talk to you.' Warming to my theme I foolishly pressed on with my attack. 'You rant and rave so much you make it impossible for anyone to speak to you rationally, if you insist on behaving like a lunatic you shouldn't complain when people treat you like one.' I realised when uttering that last remark that I had in all probability gone too far, but by then it was too late to do anything about it.

Nielsen returned to behind his desk and motioned for me to sit down opposite him. 'We will discuss this now and *I* will decide on what we do,' he said, emphasising the I, as he pushed the papers towards me across the desk.

It very quickly became apparent during the debate which followed that such was the vehemence of his opposition to my proposals that there was absolutely no chance of persuading him to consider adopting them even in a 'watered down' form. The argument raged back and forth, each of us struggling, not quite successfully, to retain our tempers, however I knew in my heart that I was fighting a lost cause. In exasperation I finally drew the meeting to a conclusion by thumping his desk and saying, 'I trust you understand that any company that denies its past hasn't got a future'. But from the expressionless look on his face I could tell I was simply wasting my time in attempting to change his opinion.

As I returned to my office I reflected on how I had been horrified to discover that Nielsen had known nothing of my previous discussions with the Public Affairs Director. On further investigation I uncovered the truth of the matter, which was that she had indeed broached the topic with Nielsen some time previously but had received a stern rebuff. Accordingly, to save her own skin she took the decision to deny all knowledge of the situation, or to acknowledge that she had previously given her approval for my actions. It was a painful but invaluable lesson in the art of industrial politics, and was one which I would never forget. In future I would make sure I always had something in writing which I could use to cover my back in times of trouble.

While this salutary experience had been a bitter lesson, worse was to follow, and it would shatter the trust I had placed in some of my colleagues. One particular incident had started rather innocuously with a telephone call from the American salvors of the *Titanic*, RMS *Titanic* Inc., a New York-based company who held the salvage rights to the recently discovered wreck. The company was headed by George Tullough, a former BMW automobile dealer who had spotted the commercial potential of recovering artefacts from the ocean floor surrounding the wreck. He appreciated that to offer for sale any personal items recovered from *Titanic* itself would lead to opprobrium for him, and would undoubtedly lead to his company being branded grave robbers. On the other hand, the same could not be said regarding the recovery and subsequent sale of lumps of coal recovered from the debris field surrounding the wreck.

The cost of recovering these artefacts had left this organisation desperately short of funds, but they had recovered several pieces of coal which they subsequently had broken up into minute pieces and were now offering for sale to the general public. Despite a huge marketing effort the initial sales had been a disappointment, and, desperate to add credibility and some sort of tacit approval to this rather objectionable activity, he looked to an association with Harland & Wolff. It was clearly their hope that marketing these unsavoury trinkets in conjunction with the name of the makers of the *Titanic* would give them some sort of cachet. My immediate reaction was that I was primarily concerned with safeguarding the valuable reputation of Harland & Wolff, and I believed that such an alliance would certainly not be in the best interests of the company. I was also mindful of my extraordinary previous encounter with Per Nielsen and was confident he would also disapprove of any involvement in such an operation. After listening carefully to what was being proposed, I compiled and circulated a written report for consideration by the Board of Harland & Wolff on my contact with Tullough and my reasons for recommending rejection of his overtures. I later assumed that as the Board had accepted my report, that that would be the end of the matter, except, unbeknown to me, my confidential report would be read by another party who would see it as an ideal opportunity to indulge in some chicanery.

Based as I was in the Technical Services division of the company I had, as a matter of routine, provided the company financial controller with a copy of my report to the main Harland & Wolff board. She had fundamentally disagreed with my opinion and, unknown to me, proceeded to make contact with George Tullough. She advised him that the company had had second thoughts on his offer and were indeed interested in exploring his proposal further. To this end, she and the purchasing manager arranged to fly to New York for a few days to meet Tullough, discuss his offer, and explore the possibility of Harland & Wolff becoming involved. Quite what they hoped to achieve from such actions, apart from a 'jolly' to New York at company expense, will forever remain a mystery to me. Particularly so given that they were both well aware of Per Nielsen's attitude to such ventures, and indeed the fact that it had been completely rejected by the Board.

As it was, a few days later the pair departed on their trip and their absence from the office was explained to anyone who happened to ask as being a few days' holiday. Perhaps the most worrying aspect of all this is the fact that here was a deliberate deception that would not have been possible without the connivance of the company general manager. The extent of this dishonesty was inadvertently discovered some weeks later. In fact, I only became aware of it when I was routinely asked by one of the invoice clearance clerks to initial my approval for payment of the invoices covering the air tickets and hotel accommodation expenses.

The financial controller had intended to approve these invoices herself, however her deceit had inadvertently been exposed by the invoice clerk, who was following the correct procedure in passing the invoices to the cost centre chief, in this case me, for approval.

Furious at their underhand behaviour and the monumental cheek of using my departmental budget to fund their week-long jaunt to New York, I immediately raised the issue with the general manager who, much to my astonishment, decided against taking any disciplinary action. Such fraudulent behaviour would, under normal circumstances, have resulted in instant dismissal for those involved and most likely criminal proceedings being instituted against them. I was simply astounded that in such a blatant case of deception the whole affair was apparently to be brushed under the carpet. For a while I did consider bringing the matter directly to the attention of the group financial director or even to the Chairman of the Board of Directors, but on reflection I decided to follow the unwritten code and say nothing. To blow the whistle on any nefarious activity would see the whistleblower being isolated and ostracised by their colleagues. They would then find themselves allocated only the most difficult and unpleasant of duties.

It is perhaps understandable, given the continual changes of direction the company had been taken on by an ever-changing cast on the Board, that self-serving greed and neglect should be evident in almost every aspect of company procedures. Scams and petty fiddles became the order of the day as senior management felt increasingly impotent in the face of such widespread deceit and corruption. Certainly, the unwritten code did not only apply to occurrences of theft or dishonesty, it applied equally to acts of violence. These were still a frequent occurrence in the testosterone-charged atmosphere that always surrounds a male-dominated environment like a shipyard.

On one occasion a particularly tiresome and obnoxious foreman had been deliberately irritating one of his colleagues for most of the day. As it turned out he was to receive his comeuppance. Several of us had advised this particular individual that it would perhaps be wiser for him to restrain his comments and not to further inflame an already tense situation, however our warnings went unheeded. During a short tea-break that afternoon this rather foolish individual was once again giving voice to his opinions. Suddenly he appeared to fly across the room, striking the wall of the port-a-cabin we were occupying with an almighty thump before sliding down it to land in a crumpled heap on the floor. In stunned silence we watched as a trickle of blood streamed from his nose and down over his chin, finally dripping onto his overalls where it slowly congealed into a dark red pool. 'I told him to shut up but he wouldn't listen,' came a voice from the opposite side of the room. 'Well he's shut up now.'

After a few minutes a low moan came from the slowly recovering victim and, as we struggled to lift him to his feet he began in a quivering voice, 'Youse all saw that didn't youse? I'm gonna' get that big bastard the sack so I am, he can't get away with that.' With that he staggered free of our supporting hands and made his way somewhat unsteadily in the direction of the Personnel Department.

Of course, in strict adherence to 'the code' nobody had seen anything and that is precisely what each and every one of us said at our subsequent interviews regarding the incident. All of us realised that this was a big boys' world we found ourselves working in, and therefore we were expected to play by the big boys' rules; those who could not simply didn't understand the game they were playing.

Ever since the early sixties Harland & Wolff had been kept solvent mainly by interventions from either the Westminster or Northern Ireland Governments, each of which provided vast injections of cash to underwrite the increasing losses. For both administrations, irrespective of whoever was in power at any particular time, the prospect of the closure of the shipyard and the loss of several thousand jobs among the largely Protestant workforce was truly frightening. The idea of some 28,000 working-class Protestants taking to the streets after suddenly finding themselves without employment, and the inevitable problems such a situation would create, simply did not bear thinking about. Northern Ireland has a long history of inter-community violence and continually hovered on the verge of civil strife. By 1966 this cycle of unrest had once again begun to fester among the population and an all-pervasive atmosphere of hatred and distrust began to take root. Despite this, successive administrations had desperately tried to rid themselves of the burden of Harland & Wolff but had failed to locate a serious buyer or anyone who would be prepared to even invest capital into the company. The appointment of John Parker as Chief Executive was, to a great extent, intended to be a signal to any potential buyers that the Government had every confidence in the long-term viability of the shipyard and its future potential. With such an influential and respected figurehead running the company, the impression the Government was anxious to create was one of assured stability and long-term success. However, the reality of the situation was somewhat different in that the Government was desperate to rid itself of what had become a massive drain on the exchequer. Harland & Wolff was an ongoing liability with little or no hope of sustainable success in the future.

To those of us engaged in the day-to-day management of the company, such financial complexities never entered our minds. For as long as most of us could remember we had lived with the mantra that, 'the yard must be competitive and cost-effective if it is to survive in today's economic climate' ringing in our ears. Time after time the workforce were berated for not working hard enough, or for not making any effort to improve our own performance. Unfortunately for those exhorting greater efforts from an essentially demoralised workforce, their rhetoric was counter-productive. After having heard their efforts denounced so often, the message simply ceased to have any effect on the workforce and was routinely ignored, particularly as the amount of duplicity and trickery going on at executive level became increasingly obvious to all.

While it must be acknowledged that John Parker certainly did bring about dramatic improvements in morale which were matched by a corresponding increase in productivity, he remained constrained in his efforts by the underlying air of despondency that had become so deeply ingrained in the very fibre of the company. This air of dejection and unhappiness was so all-pervasive that the extraordinary announcement of the shipyard's imminent sale to Norwegian shipping magnate Fred Olsen was greeted with almost complete disinterest by virtually everyone. Throughout the shipyard the general consensus of opinion was that if Fred Olsen wanted to invest in this place then he must have more money than sense. Good luck to him if it meant we still had a job for the next few years. In actual fact, Olsen had much more business acumen than many gave him credit for and he managed to strike one of the shrewdest and most audacious business deals of his long career.

During his discussions with the Government, Fred Olsen quickly realised just how anxious they were to rid themselves of the albatross around their neck that was Harland & Wolff. So desperate were the Government they were ready to accept literally almost any price offered. Appreciating just how far he had the Government over a barrel, and aware of their desperation to conclude a deal as quickly as possible, Olsen tabled a ludicrously low offer of £12 million for the total assets of the company (at that time Harland & Wolff had a book value of some £93 million). Sensing that he held the advantage in the negotiations, Olsen added several conditions to this preposterous offer. Amongst them was a request for the Government to immediately write-off some £625 million of accumulated debt. He also asked that the authorities provide a complete financial and legal indemnity to Fred Olsen against any and all other claims or liabilities however arising against Harland & Wolff prior to his takeover of the company, his final condition was that a generous development grant or 'golden handshake' of approximately £20 million be provided immediately upon his assuming control of the company. Finally, the £12 million total purchase price would be paid in instalments beginning with an initial cash payment of just £6 million.

One can only assume that he was as astonished as the entire workforce when the Government immediately capitulated to these demands and accepted his offer along its unbelievable conditions. With the benefit of hindsight it is apparent that the Government of the day would have accepted just about any offer it received for the company, no matter how ridiculous or derisory the terms. Such was their determination to divest themselves of the company that the final separation was carried out with almost indecent haste. So, after a break of almost sixty years in public ownership, Harland & Wolff once again found itself passing into private hands and looking towards an uncertain future. However, Olsen had one final ace up his sleeve which he would use to, as he put it, 'give the opportunity for all the workforce to show their commitment to being a part of a bright new future for Harland & Wolff'. In other words he wanted the workforce to invest their own cash in the new company in order to subsidise his capital expenditure and so underwrite any potential loss he might be exposed to in completing the purchase.

Like all good illusions this one was very simple in concept and was based on the genuine desire of the workforce to see a real change in the fortunes and direction of the company. It also appealed to the rational human desire to establish a greater degree of control over one's own destiny. Acutely aware of the intense desire for change, Fred Olsen shrewdly offered each employee the chance to buy shares and acquire a personal stake in what was purported to be 'their' company. Of course it was stressed that the purchase of shares in this new venture was not in any way compulsory, nor was it to be taken as a guarantee of continued employment. However, failure to grasp this unique opportunity could be regarded as an indication that the individual was not fully committed to the company and its future success. To further sweeten the pill, Olsen guaranteed that 51 per cent of the total shares available in the company would be allocated to the workforce, and therefore they would collectively retain the majority stake in the company and thus their own future.

In reality Olsen had his own selected appointees on the Board, who between them held 5 per cent of the issued share capital. Together with his 49 per cent personal holding this effectively ensured that he alone controlled the company. Faced with such a 'catch 22' situation, the majority of the employees did indeed purchase shares. However, even this supposedly free choice was cynically manipulated to ensure that Olsen got the maximum financial benefit from the sale. The shares were priced at a nominal £1 each, with no lower limit imposed upon how many could be purchased. However, manual workers were encouraged to believe that an initial purchase of 500 shares was the minimum investment that could be regarded as showing the expected level of commitment.

Similarly, foremen and junior management grades were told that only a purchase of at least 1,000 shares would demonstrate the depth of their conviction. Senior managers and levels above received the message that they were expected to purchase a minimum of 2,000 shares. In many instances, staff anxious to demonstrate their loyalty and commitment to the new company purchased double, or sometimes treble, the expected allocation, with the result that Olsen recouped nearly 50 per cent of his initial outlay almost immediately. Notwithstanding the runaway success of his share offer, Fred Olsen was keen to capitalise on every aspect of this, his latest acquisition. With the company safely under his control his attention now turned to the company pension fund, or more precisely the huge cash surplus it had accumulated over several years.

For many years Harland & Wolff had been ship owners in their own right, and with this historic background in mind the pension fund trustees were persuaded to consider re-entering the world of ship-owning by funding the construction and purchase of a bulk carrier. The intention was that this vessel would then be bare-boat-chartered, that is supplied without crew, fuel or stores, for an unspecified period to Fred Olsen Shipping at a still-to-be negotiated, but commercially attractive, daily charter rate. Such an arrangement was standard practice in shipping circles, vessels of all types are commonly offered for hire or chartered for specific voyages or periods of time. The charter rate for such vessels varies on a daily basis and is dependent on the level of demand for a particular type of vessel. Unfortunately, given the volatile nature of the business, these rates can represent either a great bargain or be extremely unprofitable for the parties concerned in the charter. Clearly not a stable investment.

It was precisely because of this volatility in the market that the directors of Harland & Wolff had decided several years previously to withdraw from all activities in the field of ship ownership or operations. To be fair, Olsen's proposal may not have been quite as risky as it sounded, particularly considering the fact that the company's order book was completely empty with no immediate prospect of it being filled. Faced with such dire circumstances, the pension fund trustees consequently agreed to the formation of a wholly owned subsidiary company to be known as Trassey Shipping, which would be the ultimate owner of the new vessel *Lowlands Trassey*.[1]

With the benefit of hindsight, it does appear somewhat strange that the shipyard's new owner, who also owned and operated a substantial fleet of vessels ranging from cruise liners to oil tankers, appeared reluctant or unable to place any new building or repair work orders with his own company. Perhaps even more telling was the fact that Olsen had recently concluded contract negotiations with a Korean shipyard for the construction of four products tankers, vessels for which the facilities at Harland & Wolff were ideally suited.

Nevertheless, faced with the prospect of imminent closure due to the empty order book, the shipyard was grateful to receive any order, whoever or wherever it came from, and construction work commenced almost immediately on *Lowlands Trassey*. Unfortunately, it wasn't long before the company ran into an unforeseen snag. Being both the ship owner and the builder inevitably produced a conflict of interest. In normal circumstances the builder strove to build the vessel to the contract price while the owner was constantly seeking ways to extract the maximum improvement to the vessel specification with no extra cost to themselves. It was Fred Olsen who once again stepped forward to provide the solution to this dilemma. His shipping company (acting under the auspices of being the primary charterer of the vessel), would oversee construction of the vessel on behalf of Trassey Shipping, for the appropriate commercial fee of course. This arrangement meant that Fred Olsen had astutely put himself in the position of having a vessel built to his precise requirements and specifications but having it financed by somebody else.

The return to ship-owning ultimately proved to be a very expensive lesson for the trustees of the pension fund. *Lowlands Trassey* operated for a few years under charter to Fred Olsen but never succeeded in returning a profit due to the incredibly low charter rate Olsen had negotiated. Just two years after her completion, *Lowlands Trassey* was sold to Fred Olsen Shipping for a price that amounted to little more than the scrap value of the steel used in building her hull. When the details of this transaction finally emerged, the reaction was one of fury among the trustees of the pension fund, who were obviously horrified to see the fund assets depleted in such a manner. Regardless of the understandable disquiet expressed at the sale of *Lowlands Trassey*/Trassey Shipping at such an enormous loss (£3.4 million), neither Fred Olsen or Harland & Wolff ever provided a precise explanation of the arrangements entered into concerning *Lowlands Trassey*/Trassey Shipping.[2]

The air of euphoria surrounding Olsen's purchase of the shipyard and the new beginning he had promised had been replaced once again by an atmosphere of suspicion and distrust. The *Lowlands Trassey* incident merely served to demonstrate what many employees had begun to suspect, that the company's true attitude towards the rank and file employees had changed to one of utter contempt and disregard for their rights and opinions. In particular, those on the lower-to-middle management grades found themselves in the invidious position of having to supervise and direct an increasingly apprehensive and disenchanted workforce while being oblivious to what was going on above them. The uneasy but all too familiar feeling of *déjà vu* had once again returned to haunt the shipyard. Had nothing changed? Would anything ever really change? Into this increasingly volatile atmosphere the last thing the company needed was the intervention of Per Nielsen, but that was precisely what it got.

Since his arrival at Harland & Wolff some years earlier, Per Nielsen had particularly disliked the Edwardian-style Main Office block but reserved a particular aversion for anything even remotely related to the history and eventual destiny of the RMS *Titanic*. Much to my regret I had crossed swords with him on this very issue already. However, on this particular day Nielsen would play his trump card. He suddenly announced the closure of the Main Office building and the relocation of all its staff to a subsidiary office complex located alongside the huge building dock. Thus, in one fell swoop Nielsen had wiped away over 125 years of company history and tradition.

Worse was to come, however, when I found myself being summoned to his office later that morning and he informed me of his decision:

> Of course as Archive Manager you will appreciate that we cannot possibly relocate the historical drawings and technical records to the new office building. I can allow you one month to find a solution to what I consider to be *your* problem, otherwise I shall have no hesitation in having the records destroyed.

I grimly noted his particular emphasis on the word *your*, and was left in no doubt whatsoever that he had every intention of doing precisely what he said.

From past experience I was only too well aware that Nielsen did not make idle threats or back-track from decisions, however unreasonable or illogical they may have appeared to anyone else. A massive logistical problem had therefore been deliberately and unnecessarily created for me, a difficult situation that was designed to challenge my ingenuity and resourcefulness to its fullest extent.

Given the circumstances and timing of this decision it was obvious that an enormous hole had been dug for me. But if I was expected to simply fall into it and admit defeat without a fight then Nielsen did not know me very well and had a lot to learn about my character. In reality a month was an impossibly short time to resolve such a huge logistical problem, except he didn't know that I had already been giving some thought to the future preservation of our vast store of archive material. Some months previously I had opened negotiations with the Ulster Folk and Transport Museum regarding the possibility of their accepting our vast drawing archive on a permanent loan basis. Under this arrangement the drawings would be transferred into their care as part of their general maritime heritage collection. The museum would be free to exploit the collection commercially if they wished to, while Harland & Wolff would still retain legal ownership and would have free access to the material as necessary. Negotiations with the museum trustees went smoothly, and within a few weeks agreement had been reached in principle for the museum to become the official custodians of our technical drawing archive. The trustees were particularly delighted at this acquisition as it represented a unique and complete record of shipbuilding in Belfast for over a century. As a source of historical reference it was unequalled throughout the United Kingdom and probably the world, as never before had any shipyard donated its complete drawing records. As such the profile of the Ulster Folk and Transport Museum was considerably elevated within the world of maritime history. I had been anxious to preserve what I considered a vital part of the company's history. The company archive was unique in that it held not only the drawings of almost every ship we had built, but also the entire portfolio of contract documents and subsidiary papers, including trials records and performance data. Taken overall this vast wealth of information would provide students of marine engineering and shipbuilding technology with an invaluable research tool, and I was determined it should be preserved at all costs.

I had learned a lot about self-preservation over the years and was determined to fight my corner if and when I had to. Harland & Wolff had seen fit to employ me as a manager and as such I would be expected to use my judgement and common sense in the performance of those duties. If I meekly acquiesced with instructions I believed to be fundamentally incorrect or damaging to the company, then I had no right to hold the position of authority I did.

Certainly it must be said that my life in the company would have been much easier had I opted for the quiet life and kept a low profile, but to adopt this attitude was totally foreign to my nature and I just couldn't do it. Perhaps I somehow felt that I still had something to prove, although just what that could be I didn't know. From joining the company as a message boy with no academic or formal qualifications I had progressed through the ranks to eventually become a departmental manager, an exceptional career path which was almost unheard of within Harland & Wolff. Unquestionably my rapid progress had caused envy and resentment among several of my contemporaries, but I steeled myself against their ill-will by recalling a quote from the late Bill Shankly, the famous Liverpool Football Club manager, 'Don't take shit from anyone' and I never have!

Astonishingly, the logistics of closing down the old headquarters and relocating all the staff and their office furniture and equipment went almost without a hitch. As the Technical Departments included all the design and drawing offices and numbered some 370 draughtsman and engineers, I had by far the largest complement of personnel and associated equipment to transfer to the new location. To further complicate matters, the work of these various departments on the construction drawings, urgently required by the shipyard trades, had to proceed without disruption. Any delay in the supply of these drawings would seriously affect the production schedule and would result in men being laid-off due to lack of work. In the end I adopted the simple expedient of creating a new office environment for each drawing office. This was done by utilising whatever spare desks and drawing boards I could beg, borrow or steal from throughout the shipyard. The operation commenced on a Friday afternoon immediately after normal stopping time and continued without a break on a shift basis over the entire weekend. In undertaking such a massive logistical exercise I had the invaluable help of a dedicated team of men, and working together we managed to complete the whole operation by 9.00 p.m. on the Sunday night.

The men under my charge had performed brilliantly and completely exhausted themselves with their efforts. I therefore felt that a gesture of appreciation from the company would be appropriate under the circumstances and so I authorised the provision of a meal of fish and chips and two cans of beer for each man. As luck would have it, the crew were just settling down to enjoy their treat when the Maintenance Director and his General Manager arrived on site to check on the progress of the operation. While I was fully aware that the drinking of alcohol on company premises was strictly forbidden in all circumstances, I had exercised my discretion and authorised it on this occasion. I explained this to the Director, adding that in my opinion the men had earned it by their efforts. I explained that I wished to express my personal gratitude in some tangible way and therefore if there were to be any repercussions I was to be held entirely responsible. I needn't have worried as, putting an arm around my shoulder, he whispered into my ear, 'I'd have done the same myself. I don't suppose you have a spare can or two knocking about?' When Monday morning dawned the entire staff of the Technical Department were able to report to their new locations without the slightest pause in operations being necessary.

Not for the first time I had managed to achieve the seemingly impossible thanks to the willing support and cooperation of a fine crew of men. As we stood together watching the draughtsmen and engineers settle in to the new surroundings we had created for them, the facilities Department foreman, Andy Gordon, universally known in Harland & Wolff as 'The Old Master', placed his hand on my shoulder. 'You know young fella,' he said, ' by doing what you did for my men you have won their respect and admiration. There's nothing you need to learn about man-management.' I allowed myself a rueful smile as I wondered how Nielsen might react to such an opinion.

When faced with such seemingly impossible challenges it is fair to say the unacknowledged (and often unrecognised) strengths and qualities of shipyard personnel come to the fore. In undertaking this relocation I was fortunate to work closely with one of the finest men I have ever had the fortune to meet. Without his help and enthusiasm the whole operation would not have gone anywhere near as smoothly, and could well have turned into a logistical nightmare. A giant of a man standing over six feet tall and built like the proverbial brick outhouse, his gruff exterior belied a heart of gold underneath. Not that Andy ever advertised that fact when it came to supervising his staff. He was also profoundly deaf, and it was this condition that gave rise to his rather unusual nickname. Issuing his instructions one morning, one of his men who had just been allocated a rather unpleasant task muttered under his breath, 'You old bastard'. Aware that something had been said but not having heard it clearly, Andy challenged the man to repeat his remark.

It is a remarkable testament to the quick wit of the shipyard that the lightning response came out as 'I said you are an old master'. Perceptive to a man, nobody else spoke, and the moment passed without further incident. However, from that moment on The Old Master became part of shipyard folklore. He joined the illustrious company of 'The Traveller', who upon completion of any task would plaintively enquire 'Where are we goin' now?' 'Dread the Winter', who would wander about the shipyard swathed in layers of clothing telling anyone who would listen that he faced each winter with trepidation, 'Nail in the Boot', who had a pronounced limp and 'Sandancer' (chancer), who would attempt any job even if he thought the complexities of it were beyond him. All these characters and hundreds more like them formed the unique camaraderie of Harland & Wolff, and it is with a smile that I remember such individuals who were, and are some of the finest men I have ever known. Today I am honoured to count The Old Master as a close and loyal friend, a friendship forged in the steel of mutual hardship under the great gantries of Queens Island.

Everyone had just begun to settle down in their new locations when the workforce were hit by two devastating body-blows in quick succession. The first was that John Parker tendered his resignation and quickly left the company. For several months it had been an open secret that he and Per Nielsen had what could be regarded, at best, as a difficult working relationship. This had gradually deteriorated to a point where the men rarely spoke to each other, something which made conducting the routine business of the company more complex than it needed to be. Considering their individual personalities this frosty relationship was hardly surprising, and regrettably the situation between them began to have a detrimental effect on the company.

Inevitably these internal divisions started to cause a ripple effect throughout the entire management structure, with the result that two distinct camps began to emerge. Predictably, in-fighting and back-stabbing between the factions worsened as the situation came to a head. It had always appeared to us that John Parker's relationship with Fred Olsen had never been anything other than excellent. But on the other hand we were not so naive as to suppose that if push came to shove Fred Olsen would not inevitably side with his fellow Scandinavian. Certainly, Nielsen appeared to have a much closer personal relationship with Olsen than Parker, and as such he was widely regarded as being little more than Olsen's puppet. Unquestionably, over the year before he tendered his resignation, Parker had become increasingly frustrated at the number of times his strategy for the company was blocked or frustrated by Nielsen, with the apparent support of Fred Olsen. It is perhaps too simplistic an explanation of his resignation to say that John Parker just became ever more aggravated and discouraged by the whole exasperating scenario. But whatever the reason for his departure, our last real hope that Harland & Wolff would somehow regain its previous reputation as one of the world's greatest shipyards departed with John Parker, and we were once again left alone to face an uncertain future.

Hard on the heels of the shock resignation of John Parker came the announcement that Harland & Wolff was to be split into seven separate operating companies, each with its own Board of Directors and financially independent from the core business of shipbuilding and heavy engineering. While each of these new companies would be regarded as a completely new business in its own right, it would ultimately be a subsidiary of a new umbrella organisation, to be known as Harland & Wolff Holdings Ltd.

By far the largest of these new entities was Harland & Wolff Shipbuilding and Heavy Engineering Ltd, who were to have the responsibility of carrying on the shipbuilding operations, still regarded as the core business of the company. The remaining elements of the shipyard – the joinery, painting, ship repair and electrical manufacturing departments – all found themselves as independent operations.

While such a neat excision was possible with these ancillary departments, the Technical Department, because of its size and diversity of operations, proved to be much more of a challenge. The newly slimmed-down shipbuilding company had no requirement for such a large complement of highly skilled and specialised Marine Engineers and draughtsmen. On the other hand, having invested vast amounts of time and money over the years in training this exceptional cadre of workers to such a high standard, the company was reluctant to discard such a valuable resource now.

Subsequently the decision was taken to split the Technical Department in two, with the reserve of the technical staff having been identified as not required by the shipbuilding company that was to form Harland & Wolff Technical Services Ltd. This subsidiary company was intended to operate as a design consultancy, offering its considerable expertise to clients across the globe. Grasping the opportunity to finally rid himself of what had become a thorn in his side, Nielsen declared that it would also be responsible for the company archives. Just three days later, two large rubbish skips appeared outside the building which now served as the headquarters of the Technical Services company. The entire archive documentation from the shipbuilding company had simply been loaded into these skips and delivered to me. I found it beyond comprehension why anyone could treat what were irreplaceable records in such a careless and cavalier manner.

I had the skips removed to part of our central stores and their contents were carefully tipped out onto large plastic sheets spread out to protect the documents. Over the next four months I spent my evenings and weekends going through these documents, cataloguing and recording every item and the historical record they contained. Eventually the task was completed and I had compiled a complete inventory of every one of the documents and drawings that had been so callously discarded. Many of the records I had salvaged were contract documentation and files of correspondence with the various ship owners. Given the nature of this documentation and the fact that they contained little or nothing in the way of drawings, I realised they would be of little interest to the Folk Museum. They were already struggling to cope with the mountain of material I had donated to them and to accept any more would be an impossibility.

It was for that reason that I turned to the Northern Ireland Public Record Office and offered them the documentation with the promise of much more at a later stage. Much to my relief they accepted these archive records into their care to ensure their safekeeping. Unfortunately, I now found myself caught between two very different, but also very distinguished institutions, both competing for the Harland & Wolff archive. Each considered themselves to be the prime custodian of the archive, and I was forced to show considerable obsequiousness to keep each organisation happy.

Fortunately, I appear to have been successful with my flattery and sweet talk as both institutions consider themselves proud custodians of what remains of the Harland & Wolff archive. However, not everything was salvaged. It is to my eternal regret that before I could rescue several thousand drawings from a storeroom, their destruction was ordered. Such pointless actions left me feeling angry and frustrated, but nevertheless it starkly illustrated the challenge I would face in seeking to preserve whatever I could of this great company's archive.

From the outset it became apparent that the staff who would form the nucleus of these new companies would have absolutely no say as to which company they had been assigned or any right of appeal should they wish to challenge their appointment. The first indication anyone received of their new terms and conditions was to be a letter sent to their home advising them of their revised employment conditions. This offer had to be accepted within forty-eight hours otherwise the employee would be deemed to have declined the offer of employment and therefore have resigned from the company.

The draconian methods by which these changes were imposed upon the workforce did considerable damage to already severely strained industrial relations. Quite why it was considered necessary to adopt such a deliberate and provocative attitude will probably always remain a mystery. Without doubt it served to erode the confidence and loyalty of the vast majority of employees, particularly those who found themselves displaced from the shipbuilding company. This feeling of isolation was reinforced by a series of directives issued by Per Nielsen; these diktats directed that only employees of the core company were allowed access to facilities such as the canteens, car parks and medical centre. In the case of the medical centre, such was the outrage among the trade unions that Nielsen was forced to immediately rescind the directive.

In spite of this enforced climb-down, Nielsen refused to accept defeat over the issue and was determined that all shipyard facilities would be denied to employees from a subsidiary company. Accordingly he introduced a procedure whereby each subsidiary company would be charged with the cost of any medical treatment provided to any of its employees. In reality this nonsensical instruction was completely ignored, much to the relief of the medical staff who had, much to their credit, refused point-blank to deny medical treatment to any person requiring it.

Regrettably, situations like those with the medical centre were becoming ever more common, and it is a sad reflection on the state of Harland & Wolff that it was allowed to develop in the first place. As the subsidiary companies found the struggle increasingly difficult, it appeared to even the most optimistic among us that there was a deliberate policy to undermine them. For example the joinery company, Harland & Wolff Outfit Services Ltd, would be asked by the shipbuilding company to tender for outfitting work on a vessel under construction, only to see the work being awarded to another contractor. The usual reason given was that the outfit services company tender was priced too high; however evidence of this was rarely provided.

Similar situations existed within each other company and led to a widespread feeling that we were not operating on a level playing field. As a result of these contemptible activities, a new buzz word began to circulate throughout the company. It was said that everything was FUBAR (Fucked Up Beyond All Recognition), and indeed it was. Instead of rebuilding a once great shipyard and safeguarding employees' jobs and futures, the entire workforce found itself playing what amounted to children's games. Unfortunately none of us were children, and struggling to earn a living in such a hostile environment certainly wasn't a game.

1. Harland & Wolff Annual Report and Accounts 1999 and 2000.
2. Harland & Wolff Annual Report and Accounts 2000 (page 40).

Chapter Nine

Over the years an enormous amount has been written and said about the RMS *Titanic*. In particular attention has focused on the position of Harland & Wolff and its involvement in the many efforts to preserve the history of what is probably the most famous vessel ever built. It would be fair to say that since the discovery of the wreck site by Dr Robert Ballard in 1985, an entire global industry has built up encompassing almost every aspect of the ship, from academic research and historical study to the disreputable business of seemingly turning the site of the disaster into little more than a macabre tourist attraction. Ever since the loss of the *Titanic* in 1912 and the subsequent public inquiries into the disaster, Harland & Wolff had adopted a strict policy of refusing to officially respond to any requests for drawings or technical information on the vessel. Certainly, while the company recognised that it could not prevent any of its employees from offering their own views, it was made abundantly clear that any such opinion or comment was to be made as a personal opinion only, and was in no way to be presented as being representative of Harland & Wolff.

The loss of *Titanic* had been little short of a tragedy for the entire workforce, particularly so for Chairman Lord Pirrie, who suffered the loss of his favourite nephew Thomas Andrews, the lead designer of the ship. The company was also deeply affected by the loss of its entire guarantee group, an almost irreplaceable set of engineers and craftsmen who were to carry out the usual minor adjustments necessary on any vessel's maiden voyage. In the light of these tragic losses and their aftermath, it is completely understandable that the company would be extremely sensitive to the issue of how it should respond to the seemingly unending requests for information. The public enquiry had totally exonerated Harland & Wolff, the design and construction of *Titanic* was sound and they bore no responsibility whatsoever for the foundering of the vessel and the tragic loss of life. Bearing this in mind, Lord Pirrie issued strict instructions that in relation to the *Titanic*, the company's official response would be one of a simple 'no comment' at all times. Unfortunately, by rigorously adhering to this policy the company unwittingly created the impression that it had something to hide. This impression, however false it was, would eventually lead to Harland & Wolff adopting a virtual siege mentality and distancing itself from all references to the RMS *Titanic*.

Following on from Dr Ballard's discovery of the wreck, Harland & Wolff once again found itself inundated with requests for copies of the technical information and construction drawings which were held in the company archives. While the company undertook to be as helpful and cooperative as possible in its response to these requests, it soon found itself facing a difficult and almost impossible situation. The former policy of a blanket refusal to assist was unquestionably no longer viable, events had moved on and modern society simply would not accept such an uncommunicative attitude from a corporate body.

This public relations dilemma was made worse by the progressively more madcap theories put forward to explain the loss of the vessel. These ranged from deliberate sabotage to the use of sub-standard and brittle steel in the construction of the hull. On one occasion the company even found itself accused of collusion with the White Star Line, the owners of *Titanic*, in a plot to swap the previously damaged *Olympic* with *Titanic* and defraud the vessel's insurers. I could see that in dealing with such sensationalism I would need to be extremely careful in any response. Unhappily, my task would be made all the more difficult by the negative attitude adopted by Per Nielsen towards the company archives, and in particular any direct association by the company with the RMS *Titanic*.

It was against this highly charged background that I found myself faced with the difficult task of formulating a policy in which Harland & Wolff could at last properly acknowledge its role in the history of the *Titanic*. At the same time it was paramount to maintain a degree of dignity and respect for all those who had perished in the disaster. It is a measure of the success of my stewardship that the general public saw Harland & Wolff as being sympathetic and sensitive to the memory of the RMS *Titanic*; we were widely perceived as taking pride in our maritime heritage and place in the industrial history of Northern Ireland. Unfortunately, that public façade was very far removed from the reality of the situation. While the company was content to shelter behind this new policy of greater openness, in truth it had absolutely no interest whatsoever in cooperating with, encouraging or even assisting any research into any aspect of the RMS *Titanic*, or indeed any of the vessels it had previously constructed. On the other hand, the company was prepared to ruthlessly exploit every opportunity it could to cash in on the insatiable demand for memorabilia associated with the *Titanic* or any other commercial opportunity. I found myself struggling to reconcile such a blatant contradiction as I set out in my task of attempting to turn our vast archives into a recognisable company asset. While I had absolutely no doubt of the value these irreplaceable archives represented to the company,

I was well aware of the difficulty I would face in convincing others of this point.

As Archive Manager I was able to exercise some influence on company policy in this regard, and right from the beginning my idea was to create a signature range of top-quality, collectable merchandise. These tasteful and superior items would not be exclusively concentrated around the *Titanic*, but would be a celebration of the complete shipbuilding history and heritage of Harland & Wolff. Unfortunately, what I had not anticipated was the secret agenda which would, at every stage in the project's development, be insidiously undermining everything I tried to create or achieve. With the benefit of hindsight it is all too obvious that the real but unspoken policy of Harland & Wolff was to deny every approach it received for assistance in the promotion of the shipbuilding heritage for which Belfast is widely recognised.

Certainly the company was very anxious to present to the public an image of being willing to offer any support it could to projects designed to promote the industrial heritage of Northern Ireland. However, behind the scenes the reality was that the company actively discouraged any such involvement and did its best to be as difficult and uncooperative as possible. I have lost count of the number of meetings I have attended, with bodies ranging from the Northern Ireland Tourist Board, to Belfast City Council, to small local historical groups, where I was required to portray a false impression of interest on the part of the company. All the while I knew full well that the company had no intention whatsoever of becoming involved. On several occasions I left those meetings disgusted at the manner in which I had lied and created the false impression that Harland & Wolff would be supportive of their proposals.

I could have resigned my position on a point of principle, but what would have been the point? The cold facts are that I chose not do so for several reasons, which, in descending order of importance are:

1.) I had a wife and mortgage to consider.
2.) The grounds for my resignation would not have been made known outside Harland & Wolff.
3.) Had I resigned I would only have been immediately replaced by a more willing conspirator.
4.) And finally, what real difference would taking such a stand have made to the situation?

In all honesty I do not feel particularly proud of the way I acted, but in the cold light of reality I had to accept I was just another employee, an employee who would be expected to carry out whatever instructions he was given to the best of his ability. Realism tells me that absolutely no good whatsoever would have come from taking a principled stand on the issue. I decided that I did not wish to make myself a martyr and could do much more good by remaining where I was. From there I could work steadily towards changing a company policy I knew to be fundamentally wrong.

In this endeavour I made some early progress with the introduction and launch of the Harland & Wolff Maritime Collection. This was a collaboration between several local manufacturers and ourselves to produce a range of fine giftware and merchandise evoking the splendour of a bygone age. The products epitomised the elegance and luxury of ocean travel and appealed to the nostalgia which is a part of all of us. Much as I loathed the idea of appearing to jump on the RMS *Titanic* bandwagon, I realised that there could be no better starting point than this most famous of vessels. I felt confident that in endeavouring to reproduce tasteful *objet d'art*, depicting the grace and sophistication of the great liner and the Edwardian age, the company's reputation for quality would be safeguarded and maybe even enhanced.

The initial product range encompassed some of the finest Irish linen napery ever produced, complemented by bone china tableware and crystal glassware faithfully recreated from the original White Star patterns, as well as those from other shipping lines. Obviously the centre of interest would be the reproductions of the items used on the ill-fated *Titanic* and, ever mindful of the need to maintain a sense of the style of this particular vessel, I ensured that only the most authentic and tasteful items would be reproduced.

Having had my fingers badly burnt in my previous confrontations with Per Nielsen, I was determined that this time I would leave him no opportunity to object to my plans. By ensuring he was kept fully up to date with every aspect of the project, I prevented him from saying that he had not been kept fully informed whenever anything went wrong.

However, I too had become wily and developed a trick or two of my own. It was clear that in taking this project forward I was placing myself out on a limb and leaving myself vulnerable to criticism, or even worse should the venture fail or produce adverse publicity. On several occasions I must confess I had severe doubts as to the wisdom of my course of action in the face of such hostility and opposition. Why was I struggling alone to preserve the company archive, I repeatedly asked myself over a series of sleepless nights. Every time the answer was the same – because nobody else will.

Without doubt my job would have been made much easier had the archive material been considered a valuable company asset. Regrettably, however, Nielsen and I came to another of our clashes. During what was to prove a particularly difficult meeting, at which the revised company structure was outlined to the

Above: 18 Typical Harland & Wolff transport fleet. This picture was taken in 1972, the lorry had been going strong since 1936.

Below: 19 Musgrave Channel basin, 1965. The Apprentice Training School is to the left behind the bow of MV *British Mallard*. This area was drained and converted into a giant building dock in 1971.

Above: 20 Typical working conditions for the men when a vessel was under construction.

Left: 21 Lowering a boiler into a vessel. This photograph illustrates the dangerous working conditions that Harland & Wolff workers endured, even when carrying out routine tasks.

Above: 22 The Victoria Shipyard of Harland &
Wolff. The ferry from the western side of the
river Lagan is docked at a small landing stage,
hidden behind the stem of the oil tanker in the
foreground. It was along the quay that I walked that
first morning in the pouring rain. I passed a Royal
Navy vessel moored alongside and saw a rating
cleaning out the inside of a dustbin.

Right: 23 Installing ventilation machinery on SS
Southern Cross.

24 Typical staging (scaffold) arrangement in Harland & Wolff. The staging was made from wood by apprentice joiners and wheeled into place. It was anchored in place by the simple expedient of a man standing with his foot on the base!

25 Lifting the funnel for a motor ship prior to its installation on the vessel. This heavy lift is controlled by the small group of men at the base of the funnel pulling on attached ropes to guide the lifting process. Many men were crushed during such operations.

Above: 26 'Deep water' outfitting basin with Thompson dry-dock and Queens Shipyard in the background.

Right: 27 Lowering the bedplate and base of a main engine into a motor ship while being guided into place by men armed with nothing more than pinch (crow) bars.

Left: 28 Installed fin on *Pendennis Castle*. Note the ramshackle staging arrangement and lack of any safety equipment. This scene is typical of working conditions throughout Harland & Wolff until the late 1980s.

Below: 29 Safety at work Harland & Wolff style: fitting a stabiliser fin to RMS *Pendennis Castle*.

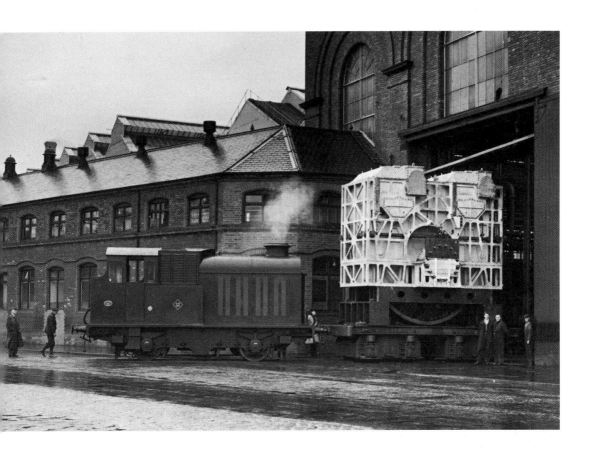

Above: 30 *Puff the Magic Dragon*, Harland
& Wolff's own engine, transporting
machinery from the Engine Works in
1965.

Right: 31 Typical working conditions
at the 'deep water' outfitting quay. No
sanitation or washing facilities were
provided.

32 The author's father (also known as 'The Sandancer') with his back to the camera laying the first keel plate for the P&O liner *Canberra*.

various departmental managers, I chanced to remark that unlike new and thus unknown ventures we were in the fortunate position of having an illustrious history as a foundation upon which to build the new company. From the thunderous expression on Nielsen's face I immediately realised I had said the wrong thing.

He thumped the table in front of him to emphasise that this was 'a new Harland & Wolff'. 'That's all very well for you to say,' I replied, 'but the general public don't appreciate or understand that, to them we *are* still the same old Harland & Wolff.' As I spoke I could see my general manager begin to nervously fidget about in his seat opposite me while signalling furiously that I should keep quiet. To be fair I probably would have done, had Nielsen not returned to the attack once more. 'It is NOT the same Harland & Wolff!' he shouted, 'This is a new and different Harland & Wolff!' Sensing that I had been presented with an irresistible opportunity to hammer home my point I calmly asked, 'In that case why didn't you change the company name then?'

It was a rhetorical question of course, but nonetheless it served its purpose admirably. Seeing Nielsen speechless for once I couldn't resist adding for good measure, 'I suppose you *do* realise that any company who denies its past hasn't got a future?' Looking directly across the table at Nielsen I was convinced that he was about to explode in fury but, much to my surprise, he chose simply to ignore the bait and merely carried on to the next item on the agenda. As the tension of our heated exchange slowly dissipated, the tone of the meeting returned to normal but I could clearly see the suppressed fury etched in his grim expression.

Realistically, I knew that while I may have won that particular battle the war was far from over, and indeed I had probably just made an even more determined and implacable enemy. As the meeting continued around me, my thoughts kept returning to our bitter exchange. I disconsolately realised that any chance I may have had of convincing Nielsen that preserving the company archives could be developed into a viable business proposition had certainly evaporated now. I had won nothing more than a Pyrrhic victory, I had indeed won that particular battle but I knew in my heart that the war had been lost. Any further attempt to explain my ideas to him face to face would be a completely pointless exercise, and so I resorted to the old Harland & Wolff memo trick. Put simply, this was to submit any contentious proposals to one's superior under cover of a memo and then simply to 'forget' to send them the actual document, as further insurance additional copies would be sent to people who could be relied upon for wholehearted support, or at the very least ambivalence. When the inevitable confrontation occurred, one would simply produce one's copy of the original memo. Here you would say that as you had received no comment or objection from the recipient, you had assumed this represented tacit approval to proceed as proposed. Clearly I couldn't rely on this subterfuge too often, but used prudently it had served as an invaluable ruse in occasionally extracting me from delicate situations. I deeply regretted having to resort to such methods, but I could see no other way of ensuring the preservation of the company archives. I had to take a stand for what I passionately believed in, otherwise I was simply deluding myself and, even worse, betraying the heritage of one of the greatest shipbuilding companies in the world.

The launch of the Harland & Wolff Maritime Heritage Collection (the name we eventually decided to give to these historical reproductions) was an unqualified success, particularly in the United States of America where it was to be showcased in such prestigious department stores as Macy's and Bloomingdale's in New York. Such was the excitement this new venture created in maritime and antiquities circles that the company soon found itself approached by a merchandising agent keen to purchase a license agreement to exclusively market the entire range throughout North America.

They saw limitless potential in the range, and to demonstrate their own capabilities they immediately arranged for me to meet with executives from QVC, the massive global television shopping organisation to discuss offering our products via their network. I was ecstatic at the amazing success I had achieved in such a short time, and began excitedly to plan all sorts of future developments by which the company could further expand on what had been so rapidly accomplished.

Pride, as they say, comes before a fall, and in my euphoria I had neglected to keep a weather eye open on the horizon – perhaps if I had I would have seen the developing storm that was Per Nielsen about to break.

I had just returned from a meeting with P&O (Peninsular & Oriental Steam Navigation Co.) in London, where I had held a series of very cordial discussions on the possibility of a joint venture involving what had proved to be their most popular vessel, the revolutionary passenger liner *Canberra*. *Canberra* had been built by us for P&O in 1965, and had entered service on the London/Australia immigrant trade route, where she proved to be a reliable and very popular vessel. Following the demise of these routes due to the plethora of air services to Australia, the *Canberra* opened up a new career for herself as a cruise liner, quickly establishing a loyal clientele who returned time and time again to enjoy the delights of an ocean voyage. Perhaps her most dramatic claim to fame was when she acted as a troop ship during the Falklands conflict. Who could ever forget the dramatic television pictures of *Canberra* in San Carlos water, disembarking troops while under fire from Argentinean aircraft? Or her emotional return to Southampton? Streaked with rust and battle-scarred, she would be affectionately christened by the troops she carried and protected as the 'Great White Whale'.

This was precisely the sort of maritime heritage I wanted to acknowledge and safeguard for future generations. Momentous events in history are but a brief moment in time, and once gone they are lost forever unless we seek to preserve their memory for future generations. Unfortunately, as I was about to discover, not everybody shared my opinion.

Sadly, like all material things, *Canberra* had come to the end of her useful life, and P&O had been forced to take the decision that she should be sent to the breakers yard. Such was the place this wonderful old vessel held in the hearts and minds of her loyal passengers that selling her to another shipping line for some further indeterminate service was not an option P&O considered. Furthermore, P&O had astutely recognised that disposing of her in the UK would be too distressing, and so her final voyage would be to a breakers yard in India. During the discussions on how P&O and Harland & Wolff could best commemorate the memory of *Canberra*, I managed to secure for the company the return of the huge brass builder's plaque which had proudly adorned the bridge front since her launch. I was delighted that P&O were happy to agree to my request, and a few weeks later the plaque duly arrived back at *Canberra*'s birthplace. Unfortunately, instead of seeing it placed on prominent display in the company's offices as I had hoped, Per Nielsen had it consigned to a storeroom as just another unwanted relic from the past.

I realised I was in trouble the minute I entered the office that morning. The general manager frantically beckoned me into his office as I walked past his door. The hairs on the back of my neck immediately began to stand up as he was never in the office until much later and it was obvious he had made a special effort to get in early that day. His opening remark confirmed my worst fears: 'Nielsen is coming to see you this morning. He is absolutely furious about the heritage collection and the way you have been marketing it and the publicity it has been attracting.' He added for good measure, 'He says it is making heavy industries look like a museum instead of a shipyard.' I was tempted to reply that under Nielsen's direction it was a bloody museum run by a dinosaur, but thought better of it for the moment. 'OK, thanks for telling me,' I said, shrugging my shoulders in resignation. 'What time can I expect the firing squad?'

He was saved the bother of replying as just at that moment Nielsen arrived and, gesturing towards the conference table in the corner of the office, indicated that I should sit down.

As was usual when he was angry the words came tumbling out in a torrent, making it rather difficult to understand precisely what it was he was saying, but I had no difficulty in understanding the depth of his anger. I had heard this stream of invective so many times before that it had almost no effect, and I had long since ceased to care, with the result that his comments went completely over my head. After what seemed an eternity the tirade ceased as he finally paused for breath, either that or he was expecting some sort of response from me. Suddenly, out of nowhere the words of the late Bill Shankly once again popped into my head, 'Don't take shit from anyone'. Quite unexpectedly, and without my being able to prevent it, I found a smile beginning to appear on my face as I leaned back in my chair. 'Quite finished are you?' I asked, 'Because I don't want to hear any more of this shit, I sent you a fucking memo about all of this, but if you are too stupid or pig ignorant to read or understand it then that's your problem.'

Nielsen sat bolt upright in his seat, stunned that anybody would have the nerve to speak to him like that, while Jim Lee, the general manager, turned a shade of grey and fervently wished he was anywhere else but here. 'Now sack me if you like and I'll see you in court for unfair or constructive dismissal but until you do I've got a job to do and I'm going to bloody well do it to the best of my ability.' Now it was my turn to thump the table, and to further emphasise my point I deliberately knocked over my chair as I stood up. Finally, as a parting shot, upon reaching the door I used an old shipyard expression to reinforce my dramatic exit: 'My money (salary) is too big to fuck about here all day.' And with that I slammed the door behind me.

From the stunned silence all about me I realised that every one of the staff present had heard my entire outburst, and as I walked back to my desk most of them studiously tried to avoid eye contact with me. They had been aware since yesterday that I was in for a rollicking and had desperately wanted to warn me; however the speed of events had quite simply overtaken them. A few of the braver souls risked giving me the 'thumbs up' or mouthed a 'well done' in my direction, but the stress of the past few minutes had had their effect and I was not quite as fearless as I appeared. Sitting at my desk I was acutely aware of a fluttering sensation in my chest, my heart was pounding as sweat trickled down my forehead and I had developed a severe headache. The normal background sounds seemed much louder than usual and the natural light in the room became much intensified to my eyes. As I sat behind my desk, trembling with the emotion of the last few minutes, I became aware that Nielsen was approaching my desk. However I needn't have worried, as he was merely making his way out and passed by without a word or glance in my direction.

I will never know if there would have been any repercussions from my outburst that fateful Friday because, two days later on Sunday 21 September, as I returned home from again working very late into the evening, I suffered a devastating stroke which would leave me blind in one eye and paralysed for several months. Obviously I cannot be certain if the unremitting pressure I was facing had any bearing on what had happened, but likewise it cannot be discounted. Recovering in hospital, the neurosurgeon responsible for my treatment endeavoured to find out just what had been the cause of my sudden illness. During the course of his investigations he discovered that I had been under a high level of stress for a long time, and also found out that my working week was rarely less than eighty hours, not including all the business travelling I did. Suddenly realisation dawned, and leaning forward he clutched my lifeless arm: 'That's it,' he declared, 'that's why you're here.' With an almost perceptible note of triumph in his voice he told me he had finally solved the puzzle before adding, 'And I bet you are not worrying about Harland & Wolff now, are you?' I had to concede that he was absolutely spot on in his assessment, I certainly was not worrying about Harland & Wolff or my job, my main concern at that precise moment in time was would I ever be able to walk again?

As my recovery slowly progressed I received several letters and cards from well-wishers and business associates, in particular one from James Cameron, the director of the blockbuster movie *Titanic*. The card was also signed by several of the film's stars and production crew, and their good wishes meant a tremendous amount to me as I struggled to recover some movement in my right side. I had worked for almost eighteen months as a technical consultant on the movie, and had become very involved in the construction of the massive *Titanic* set and the creation of the special effects, in particular those of the vessel breaking-up and sinking. When Peter Lamont, the production designer on the movie, had first made contact with Harland & Wolff he was naturally put in contact with me. I vividly recall the first words he said when we spoke: 'We want to rebuild the *Titanic*.' Having heard something similar so many times in the past, from what were usually well-intentioned but completely impractical people, I was naturally sceptical. Nevertheless, there was something in his voice that suggested this project could be very different, and I agreed to meet with him in Belfast to discuss his ideas further. 'Would tomorrow be convenient?' he asked. 'I can be on the first flight in the morning.' Peter was as good as his word; I picked him up from the airport and our long and technically challenging relationship began.

As I took him through the archive material we held on *Titanic*, he became more and more excited, asking me question after question which, fortunately, I was able to answer. 'You must meet Jim (Cameron), he will be over the moon when I tell him about you.' Not quite sure what he meant I simply smiled rather inanely while trying my best not to look totally embarrassed.

Peter telephoned the next day. 'Great news, Tom. I've told Jim all about you and he agrees you will be a vital part of the project, all I need now is to know how much H&W want for you.' A surreal image immediately popped into my head of me leaning against the bar in a seedy nightclub offering my services to any bidder. 'Sorry Peter, it doesn't work quite like that,' I laughed, 'but if you make them a good enough offer you never know.' I passed him on to the company financial controller who eventually negotiated an appropriate rate for my services. In any event Peter appeared very happy at her proposal, and she was equally surprised at just how quickly he had agreed to her terms.

Peter's telephone call marked my entry into the world of feature film making. From the outset James Cameron had insisted that every item reproduced for his epic movie had to be as accurate as humanly possible. In actual fact his wish was to recreate the *Titanic* in all its glory and splendour as it was in 1912, to take the audience back in time and to place them aboard the *Titanic*.

My contribution to this enormously difficult undertaking would be to act as technical advisor to the project, and in particular to work with the special effects technicians in recreating the actual sinking. My initial reaction to learning just how significant my part in the project would be was one of anxiety; could I provide the expertise they demanded? And yet I also felt a sense of great excitement at the prospect of such a challenge. In reality my fears proved unfounded and I needn't have worried at all. As the project gathered speed I found answering the thousand and one questions of the film production company on set in Mexico (or at the special effects studios in Los Angeles) to be an exhilarating and welcome distraction to the normal routine.

However, the eight-hour time difference between the UK and the West Coast of the United States did present a significant problem. The studio would be filming scenes while we in the UK had finished work for the day. To resolve this I decided to give Peter Lamont and Jim Cameron my home telephone number, little realising this meant I would receive telephone calls at 2.00 or 3.00 a.m. from the set asking for my advice on a particular item or area of the reconstructed *Titanic*. Despite the loss of sleep this caused on occasion, neither my wife Sylvia or I really objected to being so rudely awakened; we appreciated that in the movie industry time was money and we were only too pleased to help. Of course, building up such a strong interpersonal relationship also had its advantages in that we were privileged to see the finished movie long before it was released in the UK.

During the making of the movie several shots were sent via e-mail to my office for my opinion or comment as to the accuracy of the area in shot. On one occasion Peter suggested I should pay particular attention to a scene located in the engine room. Unsure of what I should be looking for in particular I told Peter it looked fine, with everything as it should be. Peter then drew my attention to the two figures in the background who could be seen brewing a pot of tea using steam from one of the boilers. 'Do you remember you once told me the engine room crew made tea at their workplace rather than leave the engine room? Well we put that scene in the background just for you.'

Laughing at my apparent shock he added, 'It's what we call a thumbprint and that one is yours.' I didn't fully appreciate what he meant, until he explained further that in almost every film those most involved in the production have a little scene that is specifically there to mark their contribution. In other words their own thumbprint that they know is there just for them. Obviously, such cameos are always in the background and thus pass unnoticed by almost everyone viewing the movie who are naturally concentrating on the action taking place in the foreground. Peter went on to say, 'Jim and I decided to put that in for you as our personal thanks for all your help over these past months.' I was somewhat taken aback by their thoughtfulness and generosity, while at the same time tremendously honoured that my contribution had been so highly regarded as to warrant such a special honour. When the film was released my name had also been included in the production credits, however to me my thumbprint scene is the icing on that particular cake.

A few months after the movie had been completed, Peter and I were enjoying a pleasant dinner together with the production accountant from 20th Century Fox when the topic of Harland & Wolff's fee for my services came up. I casually remarked that I had read in the press that the final cost of the movie was estimated to exceed $350 million and the studio had become rather concerned at the escalating costs. Both of them burst out laughing, 'I don't think you need worry,' said Peter, 'all you cost was $55,000 and we budgeted you at over $250,000. That's some accountant you have there. Boy its no wonder Harland & Wolff keep losing money.' What could I say? I sheepishly returned to my meal feeling rather embarrassed at what appeared to be a distinct lack of financial acumen on the part of Harland & Wolff.

The next day I made a point of going into our financial controller's office to tell her the good news that, because of her lack of commercial nous, she had cost the company almost $200,000. Not that my annoyance would have any effect, of course, as I had discovered to my amazement some time earlier that she was not actually a fully accredited accountant. Once again it was evident that success in Harland & Wolff was dependent less on 'what you knew' than 'who you knew'. Finally I began to understand the meaning of an expression I had heard frequently bandied about within Harland & Wolff, about individuals 'being promoted beyond the level of their abilities'. Here was a classic example.

During my time working on the movie with Jim Cameron and his crew I had established a personal relationship with Scott Landau, the US-based Vice President of 20th Century Fox. I had suggested to him that he might consider holding the European premiere of *Titanic* in Belfast. I had also suggested holding the after-premiere party in a marquee erected over the actual slipway used to launch *Titanic*. He and Cameron were delighted with the idea, as was Peter Dignam, the UK Managing Director of 20th Century Fox.

During this time a preview screening for charity was to be held in the presence of HRH Prince Charles and had been arranged for the Empire cinema in Leicester Square, London. In a telephone call a few weeks previously, Scott had told me that my wife and I would be his personal guests at the screening, and that he intended to use the opportunity to finally meet me personally and to discuss the logistics of the proposed Belfast premiere.

Due to the need for strict security surrounding any event attended by a member of the Royal Family, he requested that I keep news of my invitation secret but to look out for two tickets for Sylvia and I which would be sent to H&W about a week before the screening. While this was intended to be a personal invitation, I would by my attendance at the event also be a *de facto* representative of Harland & Wolff, and therefore protocol dictated that the tickets should be sent to the company rather than to my personal home address. Unfortunately, adherence to the correct code of behaviour would lead to the development of a rather sleazy and unsavoury situation.

Naturally I was aware of the forthcoming invitation, however Harland & Wolff, and in particular my immediate superior the financial controller, were not. By this time I had returned home from the hospital, however I remained too ill to travel to London for the screening and unfortunately this was not made clear to the officials at 20th Century Fox, who were by now in the process of sending out the invitations. Harland & Wolff had unforgivably failed to contact any of my business associates to inform them of my illness. Nevertheless, the tickets for the screening duly arrived; however this information was deliberately withheld from me. More importantly 20th Century Fox were also deceived, as they were deliberately not advised that I would now be unable to attend.

On the other hand, avaricious eyes had decided that my invitation to this gala event would not go to waste. The financial controller decided to take advantage of my absence by helping herself to my invitation and treating herself to an all-expenses paid junket for herself and a companion, courtesy of 20th Century Fox. Such was her greed that it never crossed her mind for a moment to consider the legality of her actions, to consult me on her intentions, or even have the common courtesy to ask 20th Century Fox for their agreement to her attendance in my place. So intent was she on arranging her deceitful tryst with her intended male companion for the evening that she completely failed to consider, let alone comprehend, the damaging impression of Harland & Wolff her disgraceful behaviour would give to the senior executives of 20th Century Fox.

It was at this point that the whole shabby business was exposed. I received a telephone call at my home from Peter Dignam to enquire why I had not acknowledged or confirmed my invitation to the screening. As I explained my personal situation to him he became increasingly angry at this deliberate attempt to hoodwink 20th Century Fox. He simply found it unfathomable that a company with a reputation like Harland & Wolff's could ever condone such behaviour. As the invitation had been a personal one, I immediately asked Peter if he would mind cancelling it. However, I asked him not to contact Harland & Wolff over it, but rather to leave that task to me.

He readily agreed to my request and it was obvious from the tone in his voice that he appreciated I had already formulated a plan of action to stop this deception in its tracks. Utilising my extensive business contacts with the airlines operating from Belfast, I discovered which flights the financial controller and her companion had made reservations for, together with details of the hotel accommodation that had been reserved. In addition to this vital information I also found out from one of my colleagues that she had made arrangements to hire a ballgown and had taken time off from the office that morning to splash out on an expensive hairdo in preparation for her trip to London. Now armed with all the relevant information, I carefully calculated the time when she was likely to leave the office for the airport and settled down to await my opportunity. About an hour earlier than I had estimated as her departure time, I telephoned Harland & Wolff and asked to be connected to her telephone. Unsurprisingly she didn't want to speak to me, but after about the second or third attempt she very reluctantly answered my call.

Just imagine her complete shock and my delight as I coolly informed her I had just cancelled her weekend fling. I hoped her intended companion would not be too disappointed when he arrived at Heathrow from Cork to find his eagerly anticipated sojourn would not be quite what he had expected. Barely disguising the glee in my voice I calmly informed her, 'I warned you what I would do if I found out you had stolen those tickets. Perhaps now you will realise that you are talking to the organ grinder and not the monkey.'

Alas her intended companion, a restaurant owner from the city of Cork in the Republic of Ireland whom she had met and been rather taken with while attending a function in my absence, was not quite so fortunate. From reports conveyed to me by several of my colleagues back at the Harland & Wolff Technical Services offices, it would appear that by the time of my call his flight to London had already departed, with the result that he arrived at Heathrow Airport completely unaware that his rendezvous had just been cancelled. To add to my delight I discovered later, from another friend in the airline business, that the gentleman concerned had found himself spending several fruitless hours kicking his heels at Heathrow as he awaited the non-arrival of his soon-to-be former benefactor. Eventually a message was relayed to him conveying the bad news about his planned weekend, and unfortunately leaving him to obtain a flight home to Cork at his own expense.

I can't imagine that the subsequent telephone conversation between the two would have been anything other than strained and acutely embarrassing for all concerned. It would certainly be difficult for her to provide a plausible explanation for the unmitigated shambles without a complete loss of any of the credibility she may have previously enjoyed.

As for the European premiere of *Titanic* being held in Belfast, I regret to say that the simple truth of the matter is that nobody in Harland & Wolff could be bothered to carry on with the work I had started. I learned later from Jim Cameron that his representative received a very curt rebuff from the company when he approached them to discuss arrangements for the occasion. Because of this lack of interest or cooperation by Harland & Wolff, the entire project collapsed. The result was that the good citizens of Belfast, and Northern Ireland in general, missed out on the opportunity to have the eyes of the world see their country in a positive light, rather than the terrible images of terrorism and violence they were so used to seeing on their television screens.

The studio executives at 20th Century Fox were shocked and dismayed at the almost hostile response they had received from the company to their approaches. However, to me such a reaction was depressingly familiar. For years Harland & Wolff had presented an image of wishing to be actively preserve its long and proud history of shipbuilding in Northern Ireland, while their actions betrayed the truth. Continually badgered by local MPs and city councillors for its support or endorsement of their various schemes, it would have been politically damaging for the company if their real attitude to such projects had been revealed.

Regrettably, this culture of duplicity and deceit was evident in almost every aspect of activity within Harland & Wolff, and no doubt played a major part in the eventual decline in the company's fortunes. It became commonplace to find lower-ranking managers submitting authorisation documentation for business journeys indicating economy class fares, however this would be altered *after* authorisation to indicate approval for the business class fare. Likewise, upon their return the travel documentation would be re-submitted for repayment authorisation of expenses incurred, however once again having been altered to indicate economy class travel. As company regulations required that all foreign travel received approval and verification at director level, the completed documentation would be finally altered after receiving the necessary director's signature to indicate the true travel costs actually incurred.

This blatant disregard for the regulations extended throughout the company, and subtle variations of this scam were carried out by several of the directors or senior executives themselves who, because of their status, were permitted by

Harland & Wolff to travel in first or business class. The usual practice simply involved exchanging their expensive ticket for the much cheaper economy class version and pocketing the difference in airfare. Alternatively, the fiddle would be adapted to enable the executives' wife or girlfriend to accompany their partner on a business trip and thus indulge themselves in a free holiday courtesy of Harland & Wolff. On such occasions it was not uncommon to discover that the business being negotiated required the executive concerned to remain in the locality over the weekend, especially if the destination was an exotic one such as the Cote d'Azur, the USA or the Caribbean.

Chapter Ten

As a consequence of my efforts to develop and preserve the company archives, and in particular those specifically related to the RMS *Titanic*, I recognised that there was enormous commercial value contained within them. Unquestionably they were priceless documents from a historical perspective, but they also represented a potential commercial opportunity for the company. While excited at such a prospect, I nevertheless quickly realised that developing this opening would require great sensitivity if the company was not to be seen as simply jumping on the *Titanic* bandwagon.

Since becoming responsible for the archives I had been introduced to several officials of the *Titanic* Historical Society Inc. (THS) based in the USA. This organisation is the world's foremost society dedicated to preserving the history and memory of this great vessel. Offering them my wholehearted assistance and cooperation with their objective, they appeared delighted that Harland & Wolff appeared at last to be prepared to open up their archive documentation to ship enthusiasts and historians alike. Adopting the most diplomatic manner I could, I advised them that while the company was considering introducing a more cooperative policy regarding access to its archives, we were still at the very early stages of considering how best to open up the company records to public scrutiny. From the outset the THS expressed a fervent desire to learn as much about the history of *Titanic* as they possibly could, and to this end I promised I would do everything I could to provide them with any information they requested. This came under the strict proviso that it must not be used for any commercial purpose whatsoever, a firm condition they readily agreed to.

The initial involvement began rather cautiously, with my agreeing merely to the hosting of a visit by some members of the THS to the company. This came under the guise of it being nothing more than a normal company visit. For several years the Belfast City Corporation had provided tours of the city by omnibus, and as the Queens Road which ran through the heart of the shipyard was a public thoroughfare, Harland & Wolff, despite its unwillingness to acknowledge the fact, found itself a *de facto* site of historical interest. Using this subtle expedient as a cover for my activities, I was able to welcome the first official party of American *Titanic* enthusiasts to the company. It was a particular honour and pleasure to give the party a personal tour of the shipyard, and in particular the areas which had participated in the construction of the RMS *Titanic*.

Such was the degree of importance I attached to this ground-breaking event that I had made arrangements for the flag of the United States, together with the Union Jack and H&W company flags, to be flown from the company flagpoles.

With the assistance of the Rigging Department, whose responsibility it was to carry out such operations, I arranged for the three flags to be raised just prior to the arrival of the THS party and before Nielsen had a chance to ask any questions. As it turned out everything went as planned until lunchtime when Nielsen, on his way to lunch, noticed the flags fluttering proudly in the breeze, but by then it was too late for him to raise any objections.

Over the ensuing months the association between H&W and the THS grew, to the extent that I felt confident enough to suggest that the society might consider holding its annual convention in Northern Ireland. Much to my delight this suggestion was enthusiastically received, and working together we proceeded to put in place the necessary arrangements to make the trip a success. From my personal perspective it was vitally important to ensure (both from a public relations point of view and also as a foray into the world of tourism) that the convention be a success. Although it had never been part of my remit, I considered the advancement of Northern Ireland as a tourist destination complementary to my activities on behalf of Harland & Wolff. These of course were activities which by their very nature generated a fair degree of publicity anyway. Of course I still had the problem of how to broach the news of this event with Per Nielsen, and hopefully ensure that he at least didn't show outright hostility to the whole enterprise.

Fortunately enough, fate would play into my hands in the shape of a major financial dispute the company was having with the Ministry of Defence, for whom we were constructing a fleet replenishment vessel. The length and complexity of these financial negotiations occupied much of Nielsen's attention at that particular time, and so I was able to simply gloss over many of the details of the forthcoming visit when he asked for further clarification. At the same time I was still very much aware that I was skating on extremely thin ice, and one slip on my part could see the whole trip being cancelled by Nielsen without any hesitation. However, as it turned out the arrangements progressed smoothly, and Harland & Wolff found itself acting as official convention hosts. We duly welcomed the *Titanic* Historical Society and its members to the company as honoured guests. For me the event represented a personal triumph, as on previous occasions the THS visits to the company had been at my personal invitation only. However, this time they were here as official guests of the company and the task of making their visit a success was infinitely less stressful than had previously been the case. In the end the convention was an immense success, with the highlight being the gala dinner held in the Harland & Wolff main function suite, which coincidentally had also been used to hold the launch reception for the *Titanic*. To add a further touch of poignancy to the evening I had arranged for the dinner to take place on 14 April and to incorporate the menu available aboard the *Titanic* on the night it tragically sank. The gala dinner turned out to be a wonderful success far beyond my expectations, and proved to be a very emotional evening for our guests, who were overwhelmed to find themselves in Harland & Wolff on the anniversary of the sinking of the RMS *Titanic*.

Although we were commemorating a tragedy, we were all determined to enjoy ourselves, and I had arranged for musical selections to be played during dinner by the regimental band of the Royal Irish Regiment, whose rousing regimental march contains a raucous yell as part of the music. Suffice to say our American visitors were enthralled by this, with the result that the band were compelled to perform several encores of their march. The band seemed to enjoy the ever more enthusiastic yells emanating from all corners of the room. The evening had been attended by the Head of the Northern Ireland Tourist Board and a representative of The United States Consul in Northern Ireland, and I was honoured and delighted to receive their congratulations on organising such a splendid event. Despite my obvious pleasure that the evening had gone so successfully, it was nevertheless disappointing to note that none of the directors or senior executives of Harland & Wolff had felt obliged to represent the company, and it was left to me to make whatever excuses I could to explain their very obvious absence.

The officers and members of the Titanic Historical Society were so delighted with their experience in visiting Harland & Wolff that they returned the following year to once again hold their annual convention in Belfast, where they also took the opportunity to visit the company as my guest. However, unbeknown to them, each time I hosted them (apart from the gala evening) I had done so without the official blessing of Harland & Wolff. Per Nielsen had accepted that the convention visit had been a success, however he did not anticipate that it would ever be repeated and was therefore annoyed to learn that a return visit had been requested. He had clearly hoped that the first visit would be the end of it, however he had been out-manoeuvred and further visits were very much on the cards. To counteract this, as a damage limitation exercise he imposed strict conditions on all subsequent visits.

These, in essence, were that no visits would be allowed access to any current production area. To ensure that this was strictly adhered to, visitors would only be granted admission during the weekend or after the usual weekday finishing time. As a final condition, absolutely no photography would be permitted either of a production area or inside one. However, this last condition was in essence quite unnecessary as these areas were of little interest to historical enthusiasts. Nevertheless, the imposition of these petty restrictions did present me with some rather awkward moments when I attempted to explain the company's activities. This had to be done while simultaneously denying anyone the opportunity of observing them.

These tours of Harland & Wolff became such a success that I found myself being besieged by local (and indeed international) historical groups with requests to visit the company and enjoy the same hospitality as the American enthusiasts had received. To this day I am proud to say that all of the groups who were afforded the opportunity to visit Harland & Wolff thoroughly enjoyed the experience, but perhaps more importantly they never had any inclination that their visit was anything other than officially supported by the company.

In truth these visits had to take place in my own free time without any official support from the company, and to this end I am eternally grateful to those of my colleagues who willingly volunteered their assistance and time to support my endeavours.

The stark realisation that I really was operating almost entirely without any meaningful form of backing came in April 1995. At this time I received an invitation to provide the keynote address at the Titanic Historical Society Convention in Long Beach, California. In compliance with company procedures I duly submitted a written request for permission to attend the event to Per Nielsen, however even with my previous experience of his attitude to such things I was shocked by the tone of his response.

While permission would be granted for me to attend the event I could not do so as an official representative of Harland & Wolff. I would have to take annual leave to cover my period of absence from the company and would be required to pay my own travel and accommodation costs. Furthermore, I was forbidden to seek any tourist board material in relation to Northern Ireland or to distribute any literature about Harland & Wolff or its associated companies. Naturally I was distressed at this attitude, nevertheless my determination to attend the event had been equally strengthened. I reasoned that if indeed I was to go in my own free time then Nielsen had absolutely no right to restrict what I did, and therefore I would do precisely as I pleased.

I did have one ray of hope, however. Shortly before my departure the then Finance Director asked to see me in his office. He had always been very supportive of my efforts to promote the heritage of Harland & Wolff and had been appalled at what he had observed happening to me as I struggled to make progress; the debacle over my trip to California had been the last straw. Confidentially I was told that my trip to California would be regarded as official company business and I was to consider myself to be representing the company. Unfortunately I needed to hear this reassurance from Nielsen himself, and while I was appreciative of the Finance Director's comments and his tacit support, I reluctantly informed him that I could not consider representing the company in the covert manner he suggested.

To resolve the issue and to fulfil my promise to my American hosts, I indeed utilised some of my annual leave, and my wife and I travelled to the United States where we were enthusiastically welcomed by everyone we met. I duly delivered a presentation on the history of Harland & Wolff and its place in the development of world shipbuilding which to my great surprise received a standing ovation.

At that moment any lingering doubts that I had done the right thing in accepting the invitation immediately evaporated into thin air. Little did I realise that, as I stood there proudly chronicling the history of the company, the institution that had been Harland & Wolff, 'shipbuilders to the world', had only a few short years left to live.

Today almost all the land once occupied by Harland & Wolff has been sold off to various property development interests, although even these apparently straightforward transactions have been shrouded in controversy. It is widely but incorrectly assumed that Harland & Wolff are the owners of the land it occupies: this is not the case. The land is in fact owned by the Belfast Harbour Commissioners, which is a public trust and is therefore merely the *de facto* owner, representing the citizens of the City of Belfast. The Harbour Commissioners act as landlords who have simply leased the land to Harland & Wolff, solely for the purposes of shipbuilding and related activities. This seemingly innocuous clause is nonetheless of vital importance as it prevents Harland & Wolff or anyone else from carrying out any other form of business activity on the site. Under normal circumstances it would present a huge obstacle to any redevelopment plans.

A few years after his takeover of Harland & Wolff, Fred Olsen began fresh negotiations with the Harbour Commissioners, ostensibly with the intention of renewing the existing leases for the land then occupied by the company (comprising approximately 350 acres situated on the east bank of the river Lagan and close to the centre of Belfast). A considerable obstacle to Fred Olsen's plans for the use of this land was the restrictive covenant which stipulated that the land be used for industrial purposes only. However, even this apparent obstacle was circumvented. This was done by persuading the two local Government ministers responsible that if the company was permitted to sell its leasehold interest in 80 acres of this land, and was allowed to develop it for commercial use, then the estimated proceeds[1] (approximately £19 million) would go to securing the future of the shipyard. This influx of funds would theoretically be earmarked for streamlining Harland & Wolff's operations and for securing its future as a major employer in Northern Ireland. The ministers were further persuaded of the merits of the company's case by the fact that the proposed deal was costing the exchequer absolutely nothing; all funding was being provided by Fred Olsen. Furthermore, to deny what was effectively a simple change in the terms of the existing lease would be unreasonable, and could unnecessarily jeopardise the company's future. Opponents of the proposed arrangement argued that this amounted to nothing more than a land-grab and sell-off of public assets, however all opposition was swept aside and the controversial deal was duly approved.

Under the insistent direction of Per Nielsen, the shipyard facilities had been greatly contracted, resulting in vast tracts of the site being left abandoned and obviously surplus to any future requirements for shipbuilding. Fred Olsen, rather than simply surrender this surplus land back to the Harbour Commissioners, successfully renewed the lease on the entire site for a further 112 years (until 2114). These secret arrangements caused some disquiet in the Northern Ireland Assembly, and the Committee for Regional Development held a series of meetings to consider the proposals and hear evidence on the matter.[2] While considerable doubt was expressed by several public representatives on the intrinsic worth of the proposals, the investigation failed to produce any sustainable objections.

With the Northern Ireland Assembly scrutiny now out of the way, negotiations with the Harbour Commissioners were swiftly brought to a conclusion. Fred Olsen immediately established a new property company, Ivy Wood Properties Ltd, specifically to oversee the management of Harland & Wolff Properties Ltd, the branch which had previously controlled the company property portfolio. This transaction in itself became the subject of further controversy when Ivy Wood Properties purchased the property rights of H&W Properties Ltd for £46 million. These interests consisted essentially of the new long-term leases and were paid for by a reduction in inter-company debt to Fred Olsen of some £16 million, the absorption by Fred Olsen of an external bank loan of £25 million, and the repayment of £5 million long-term debt owed by H&W Properties Ltd, thus giving the net purchase price of £46 million.[3]

Several current and former employees found this action inexplicable, particularly as the transaction had been cash neutral. Their reservations were not allayed when all shareholders in Harland & Wolff were offered the opportunity to invest in the new property company. The terms offered were extremely unattractive, perhaps deliberately so, and accordingly the offer went largely un-subscribed. Some months later Ivy Wood Properties began to sell off their interest in large sections of the site to various property developers for amounts in excess of £100 million. Astonishingly enough it would appear that Fred Olsen, through his property company, had managed to dispose of large tracts of land at a vast profit without any apparent benefit to either the shareholders of Harland & Wolff or the citizens of Belfast.

Many questions remain concerning the particulars of these transactions and the role played in them by certain individuals, and disquiet remains among several public representatives that their widely expressed concerns have not been fully addressed. In presenting his evidence to the Government of Northern Ireland's Assembly Committee for Regional Development on Wednesday 10 April 2002, the then Minister for Regional Development, Peter Robinson, faced close and intense questioning over the matter.

To this day there is public anger; how was it possible for the rights to the occupation of leasehold land and property to be sold by anyone other than the actual landowner? And further, how it was possible for Harland & Wolff's land interests to be disposed of in such a calculating manner? In a further twist to this already convoluted series of events, it has since been revealed that one of the property companies involved in this multi-million pound redevelopment of the 'Titanic Quarter' (as the area has now become known) is Harcourt Developments, a multi-national property and investment group. Intriguingly, or perhaps embarrassingly for Harcourt Developments, a senior member of its Board of Directors, Irish businessman Phil Flynn, subsequently found himself at the centre of much controversy over his alleged links to Sinn Fein and the IRA. Although suspected of being a finance officer for the IRA in the seventies by the Irish authorities, he was later cleared of the charges by a Dublin court.

In December 2004 the IRA were implicated as being responsible for the largest bank robbery ever to take place in the United Kingdom. The head office of the Northern Bank in Belfast was robbed of some £26 million pounds. In the police investigations into this audacious crime, large amounts of cash were recovered from the premises of several companies and individuals with which Mr Flynn had some association. While no evidence has ever been produced directly linking Mr Flynn to any illegal activity, police investigations in Great Britain and Ireland into the precise circumstances surrounding these discoveries remain ongoing. In any event, Flynn nevertheless decided to resign from his position as Chairman of the Bank of Scotland's Irish branch and also from several other directorships he held, including that at Harcourt Developments. The fact that the premises of a company in which he was a major investor had been raided as part of an IRA money laundering investigation obviously caused Flynn great personal embarrassment and left him in an untenable position.[4]

As a postscript to these events, just three months after the new leases had been signed Harland & Wolff announced plans to make almost all of its workforce redundant, leaving just forty-five manual workers on its payroll supported by a small number of white collar staff. Naturally the unions reacted with outrage and accused the company of acting in an underhand and despicable manner. Those who had opposed the deal in the first place felt vindicated and believed that Fred Olsen was indulging in nothing less than property speculation at the cost of people's occupations. To add further fuel to the already intense fire surrounding these developments, a few weeks later Harland & Wolff's parent company, Fred Olsen Energy ASA, announced it was planning to sell its rights to a further 200 acres of this land for a commercial development to be known as the 'Titanic Quarter'.

For my own part, after suffering a stroke of such debilitating intensity I was forced to retire from the company I loved. I nonetheless still retain an active interest in ships and shipbuilding and have been fortunate to have had four books published which have achieved worldwide sales. In this respect fate once again played a significant part in influencing events; I had been approached during my work on the movie *Titanic* to write a book on the construction of the ship itself. At that time I simply had neither the time or the inclination to do so and put the subject completely out of my mind. Suddenly, after suffering the stroke I found myself with time on my hands and as a course of therapy I was encouraged to put my thoughts down on paper. This would prove much more difficult than I had first imagined, as my right side was completely paralysed and, being right-handed, I was unable to hold a pen let alone write!

It was at this point that my dear wife Sylvia came to my rescue and purchased a computer for me to use as my writing medium and, with her encouragement and using only the index finger of my left hand, I started to compile my first book: *Anatomy of the Titanic*.

The publisher who had initially approached me was willing to accept my draft manuscript and to publish it. From that humble beginning I have had published *The Wallchart of the Titanic*, followed by *Ships of Harland & Wolff*, *Designs from the Shipbuilding Empire*, and finally co-authored *Titanic and her Sisters; Olympic and Britannic* with respected authors Michael Sharpe and Leo Marriott.

In June 2004 I was privileged and delighted to be awarded an MBE in Her Majesty the Queen's Birthday Honours List, the citation reading, 'For services to the *Titanic* and maritime history'.

It is my fervent hope that perhaps all that I worked for during my years with Harland & Wolff has been of some value after all. The tremendous heartache and pain I endured during my struggle to preserve the history and archives of this great company will be worthwhile if historians, and anyone else interested in the history of ships and shipbuilding, view them as being worthy of preservation. Sadly, and perhaps revealing much about the attitude of the company towards the preservation of its unique history, out of all the hundreds of messages of congratulations I received on my award of the MBE, none came from Harland & Wolff.

Working in Harland & Wolff was undoubtedly a difficult, dirty and dangerous occupation. However, it would be grossly unfair to give the impression that it was not without moments of humour, sometimes black, but nevertheless it created good companionship. The company was very much like an extended family, and like all close relationships some were friendly while others bordered on the hostile. For me, my career in Harland & Wolff provided me with a unique education in the school of life and taught me to view events from a more philosophical perspective. Harland & Wolff had its characters, both villains and saints, each and every one of them a unique product of their environment, and yet they all somehow found an analogous figure in society outside this closed environment. Many times I have been asked 'would you do it all again?' and my answer is always the same: 'without a moment's hesitation or doubt'. Perhaps it was the hardship which each of us faced every day that engendered such a strong bond between us, a bond which in itself became the instrumental factor in forging such strong personalities. Certainly, the humour and camaraderie among the workforce was unusually close for such a large organisation, and the unspoken bond that it produced was an irreplaceable and underlying source of strength to each and every one of us. Some of the incidents were nothing short of hilarious while others were deeply tragic. As a finale to my story, please allow me to share some of these moments with you.

My story relates to the outfitting process of a tanker built for British Petroleum, a tanker which unfortunately must remain nameless as the Chief Engineer in question could be easily identified from the following account. It had been an unusually hot day in Belfast, and the outfitting quay where the vessel was moored had taken on the aura of a tropical location with a heat haze visibly shimmering above the baking steel deck. The conditions in the engine room were almost intolerable as a 'basin trial', which involves running the vessel's main engine for an extended period, had been taking place since the previous evening. To escape this stifling atmosphere the Chief Engineer had taken advantage of a short break in monitoring the engine performance to enjoy a brief rest in the outside air and have a well-earned cigarette. As a relief from the sweltering heat he had rolled his heavy denim boiler suit down to his waist and seated himself on a convenient bollard, with his feet up on the adjacent guard rail he proceeded to make himself comfortable. Unfortunately he was spotted by a manager who had a reputation for hounding the employees for no particular reason other than to exercise his authority. Storming across the deck, he approached the startled Chief Engineer and, without giving him a chance to speak, commenced to give the hapless individual the mother and father of all bollockings, all in a voice loud enough for those of us within the vicinity to appreciate its severity. After a tirade seemingly lasting several minutes, in which the startled Chief Engineer said nothing, the officious manager ended his harangue by saying, 'Right now I want your name and board (personnel) number before I personally kick you off this ship!' To which the Chief, without rising from his seat or raising his voice. calmly replied, '– –, Chief Engineer of British Petroleum, now fuck off and annoy somebody else!' Exit one very deflated manager to hoots of laughter from us minions.

In a similar vein, another manager had apparently developed an aversion to any member of the workforce standing about for any period of time. Rather than ascertain why the person was standing there, he would rush up to the individual and demand that they 'Circulate, circulate'. All was well until one morning, as he made his usual inspection, he happened to notice several mysterious painted signs which adorned many areas of the deck and superstructure of the vessel.

Each of these strange signs comprised the figure 8 contained within a circle. Unable to fathom the meaning of these bizarre symbols, he called his foreman for assistance whereupon he was advised that they represented a circle surrounding the number eight, in other words his precise instruction of 'circle eight'.

During the construction of the first of the two giant cranes that dominate the Harland & Wolff site and the Belfast skyline, the old adage 'don't mention the war' inadvertently caused an awkward moment. The erection of the cranes was overseen by engineers from the manufacturer Krupp-Ardelt, the famous German engineering company well known for its munitions work during the Second World War. The German engineers staff were provided with office accommodation and facilities within one of the shipyard drawing offices. They were also allocated the services of a clerk to assist with familiarisation with the shipyard site and its various departments. Naturally enough a close friendship developed between the clerk and the chief engineer and they enjoyed each other's company on social evenings outside the confines of Harland & Wolff.

Unfortunately for both parties, the history between our two nations would lead to an uncomfortable moment for them both. Before commencing his service in Harland & Wolff, the clerk had been an air crew member of Bomber Command. However, as he had been wounded and probably traumatised by his experiences, he rarely spoke about those times, with the result that his past was largely forgotten about. On this particular evening both gentlemen were relaxing when a discussion began on the merits of Germany and the UK, which led to the German engineer enquiring, 'Have you ever been to Germany?' Came the unguarded reply, 'No, but I've flown over it at night.' After a few moments of embarassed silence both men thankfully appreciated the humour of the situation and remained firm friends. The clerk never did visit Germany.

In early 1981 Harland & Wolff received an order from Shell for the construction of two liquefied petroleum gas carriers. These specialised vessels were designed to carry their highly volatile cargo at temperatures in the region of -165°C, and as such their cargo tanks needed to be insulated from the hull using a combination of polyurethane foam and plywood. This combination of insulation materials presented the problem of how to ensure a secure and effective bond could be made to the vessel's structure. After much trial and error a system of epoxy resin was developed which proved ideal for the task. Unfortunately, this in itself presented difficulties in that the resin had to be applied in strictly controlled conditions and in an exact sequence of operations, not least because of the explosive nature of the chemicals and in particular the vapour given off during the curing or setting process.

Anyone required to work on the construction of these vessels had to attend a number of safety demonstrations to make sure they understood the nature of the hazard. For example it was expressly forbidden to have on board any form of smoking material, especially cigarette lighters or matches. One such safety demonstration was intended to provide an illustration of this danger, alas as events turned out things did not go quite as planned.

On the morning of the demonstration several of us had gathered in the Apprentice Training Centre for a presentation on the dangers of exposing these materials to a naked flame. Before us on a long table was a covered container which we were advised contained only a small amount of the resin, the object of the illustration being that even a tiny amount of this material could produce a spectacular explosion if ignited accidentally.

After what felt like an interminable lecture on the hazards of working in enclosed environments with petro-chemicals (most of us had completely lost interest after the first fifteen minutes), the safety officer at last arrived at the point we had all been eagerly anticipating, actually exposing the resin to a naked flame. Donning a thick leather apron, gauntlets and goggles, the safety officer lifted the cover off the container and dropped a lighted cigarette into the resin… nothing…the cigarette fizzed for a few moments and was then extinguished as it slowly sank below the surface of the resin. After a few moments the safety officer lit another cigarette, and after several furious puffs to produce a large glowing ember he dropped this into the mixture only to see the same result.

By now several giggles were audible in the room as the by now hugely embarrassed safety officer struggled to maintain his credibility. Removing his goggles and gauntlets he approached the container and, bending over it to get a better look, he fatally gave it a shake. With a mighty flash and fearsome boom the mixture at last ignited, causing the hapless safety officer to shoot backwards hidden by a pall of black acrid smoke. Everyone in the room sat in stunned silence for a moment while the smoke cleared and the unfortunate victim staggered to his feet. Approaching the bench he tried to regain his composure by attempting to carry on where he had left off. Alas his efforts were to be in vain as paroxysms of laughter began to ring around the room. Unknown to him he stood before us with a blackened face and minus his eyebrows, while small wisps of smoke curled upwards from what remained of his fringe.

The shipyard lavatories and the various uses they could be put to played a major role in our working lives. A favourite prank was setting fire to the newspaper some unfortunate was reading on the toilet then listening to the frantic efforts to extinguish the flames. With trousers round ankles the victim was horribly exposed and thus vulnerable to the full-blooded water bomb. This latter effect was accomplished by the simple expedient of filling a bag from a large sliced loaf with ice-cold water, and from an adjacent cubicle reaching over into the next and dropping the missile onto the unsuspecting victim. A particularly cruel way for this activity to end was for some unfortunate individual to fall asleep while seated in a cubicle (this is not as unusual as it sounds). This usually involved the older members of staff who had indulged in a satisfying 'liquid' lunch at the local hostelry and then retired to sleep off the after-effects.

Having identified a suitable victim the perpetrator would unreel the fire hose from its holder in the hallway and place the end under the cubicle door. Retreating to the safety of the hallway, the architect of the prank would proceed to open the water valve as far as possible with the result that a tremendous jet of water would blast around the enclosed space and thoroughly soak the hapless victim. Unfortunately, on some occasions this practical joke went horribly wrong, resulting in the unfortunate victim suffering cuts and bruises from the end of the flailing hose as they struggled to escape the raging torrent.

'We worked hard and we played hard' is a very appropriate metaphor to describe working in Harland & Wolff. Certainly my life has been enriched by the experience I gained in the many years I worked there. I count myself fortunate indeed to have had the privilege of working alongside men (and women) to whom the name Harland & Wolff meant they were part of an exceptional and extraordinary group of people who built some of the world's finest vessels. While it is true to say that in my own mind I had become something of a prophet without honour, I nonetheless look back on my achievements with a certain amount of pride. It has always struck me as odd that I should have received recognition from my country in the award of the MBE and yet no acknowledgement was ever received from Harland & Wolff. As time has passed perhaps the saddest aspect of this has been that since I left the company I have had the distinct impression of being ostracised by them.

I would have loved to have been invited back on occasion, if only as a courtesy, but as time passed I became tired of waiting and was left to wonder what I had done to merit this rejection. This is not being arrogant, but I have always worn my heart on my sleeve and it is fair to say that a chance remark I overheard about me sums up my feelings on the events exactly; 'I think it broke his heart'.

It has not been my intention to tell my story as one of rancour and regret for the time I spent employed by Harland & Wolff. However, I would not be human if I did not feel a certain twinge of regret at how things have turned out. Life has, of course, moved on and I frequently find myself contacted by various organisations asking for my help and advice on Harland & Wolff, and of course the *Titanic*. Today I am regarded as one of the world's leading experts on the history of shipbuilding and am much in demand for my expertise and advice, which is a situation I never fail to find remarkable and humbling for a boy from the back streets of Belfast.

1. Northern Ireland Assembly – Committee for Regional Development. Minutes of Evidence 27 March and 10 April 2002.
2. *Ibid.*
3. Harland & Wolff Annual Report and Accounts 2002.
4. *Belfast Telegraph* report, June 2005.